M000101880

The Cambridge Introduction to
Thomas Mann

Nobel Prize-winner Thomas Mann (1875–1955) is not only one of the
leading German novelists of the twentieth century, but also one of the
few to transcend national and language boundaries to achieve major
stature in the English-speaking world. Famous from the time that he
published his first novel in 1901, Mann became an iconic figure, seen
as the living embodiment of German national culture. Leading scholar
Todd Kontje provides a succinct introduction to Mann's life and work,
discussing key moments in Mann's personal life and his career as a
public intellectual, and giving readers a sense of why he is considered
such an important – and controversial – writer. At the heart of the
book is an informed appreciation of Mann's great literary achievements,
including the novel *The Magic Mountain* and the haunting short story
Death in Venice.

Todd Kontje is Professor of German and Comparative Literature at the
University of California, San Diego.

Thomas Mann in Lübeck, 1926. Buddenbrookhaus Lübeck. Reprinted with the generous permission of the Buddenbrookhaus Lübeck

The Cambridge Introduction to
Thomas Mann

TODD KONTJE

CAMBRIDGE
UNIVERSITY PRESS

CAMBRIDGE
UNIVERSITY PRESS

University Printing House, Cambridge CB2 8BS, United Kingdom

Cambridge University Press is part of the University of Cambridge.

It furthers the University's mission by disseminating knowledge in the pursuit of education, learning and research at the highest international levels of excellence.

www.cambridge.org
Information on this title: www.cambridge.org/9780521743860

© Todd Kontje 2011

This publication is in copyright. Subject to statutory exception and to the provisions of relevant collective licensing agreements, no reproduction of any part may take place without the written permission of Cambridge University Press.

First published 2011

A catalogue record for this publication is available from the British Library

Library of Congress Cataloguing in Publication data
Kontje, Todd Curtis, 1954–
   The Cambridge introduction to Thomas Mann / Todd Kontje.
      p.   cm. – (Cambridge introductions to literature)
   Includes bibliographical references and index.
   ISBN 978-0-521-76792-7 – ISBN 978-0-521-74386-0 (pbk.)
   1. Mann, Thomas, 1875–1955 – Criticism and interpretation.   I. Title.
   PT2625.A44Z73244 2011
   833´.912–dc22
   2010034948

ISBN 978-0-521-74386-0 Paperback

Cambridge University Press has no responsibility for the persistence or accuracy of URLs for external or third-party internet websites referred to in this publication, and does not guarantee that any content on such websites is, or will remain, accurate or appropriate.

Contents

Thomas Mann (1875–1955)

1875	June 6. Paul Thomas Mann born in Lübeck as second of five children (Heinrich 1871; Julia 1877; Carla 1881; Viktor 1890)
1891	October 13. Death of father, Senator Thomas Johann Heinrich Mann
1892	Spring. Mother Julia Mann moves with younger children to Munich; Thomas remains in Lübeck
1894	March. Mann completes high school and moves to Munich
	October. First novella published (*Fallen*)
1896	October. In Italy until April 1898
1898	Spring. First collection of stories published (*Little Herr Friedemann*)
1901	October. *Buddenbrooks: The Decline of a Family*
1903	February. *Tonio Kröger*
	Spring. *Tristan* (second anthology of short fiction)
1905	February 11. Marriage in Munich to Katia Pringsheim
	November 9. Birth of daughter Erika Mann
1906	November 18. Birth of son Klaus Mann
1909	March 27. Birth of son Angelus (Golo) Mann
	November. *Royal Highness*
1910	June 7. Birth of daughter Monika Mann
	July 30. Suicide of sister Carla
1912	October–November. *Death in Venice*
1914	November. Essay: "Thoughts in War"
1918	April 24. Birth of daughter Elisabeth
	October. *Reflections of a Nonpolitical Man*
1919	April 21. Birth of son Michael
	April. *A Man and his Dog*
1922	October–November. Essay: "The German Republic"
1924	November. *The Magic Mountain*
1926	April. *Disorder and Early Sorrow*
1927	May 10. Suicide of sister Julia

1929   December 10. Awarded Nobel Prize for Literature
1930   April. *Mario and the Magician*
        October 17. "Address to the Germans: An Appeal to Reason"
1933   January 30. Adolf Hitler declared German Chancellor
        February 11. Mann leaves Germany on lecture tour; exile in Switzerland and southern France begins
        October 5. *The Stories of Jacob*
1934   March. *Young Joseph*
        May–June. First trip to USA
1935   June–July. Second trip to USA
        June 30. Private dinner at White House with President Roosevelt
1936   October. *Joseph in Egypt*
        November 19. Granted Czech citizenship
        December 2. German citizenship revoked
        December 19. Honorary doctorate of Bonn University revoked
1937   January. Open letter to Dean of Bonn University; public break with Nazi Germany
        April. Third trip to USA
1938   February–July. Fourth trip to USA
        September. Begins guest professorship at Princeton University
1939   December. *Lotte in Weimar*
1940   October. *Transposed Heads*
1941   January 14–15. Guest of President Roosevelt at White House
        March. Moves from Princeton, New Jersey to Pacific Palisades, California
1943   December. *Joseph the Provider; The Tables of the Law*
1944   June 23. Becomes US citizen
1945   May. Lecture in Washington DC: "Germany and the Germans"
1946   April. Emergency operation for lung cancer in Chicago
1947   October. *Doctor Faustus*
1949   April. *The Story of a Novel*
        May 21. Suicide of son Klaus
        July–August. First visit to Germany since 1933
1950   March 12. Death of brother Heinrich
1951   March. *The Holy Sinner*
1952   June. Final return to Europe
1953   April. Private audience with Pope Pious XII
        June 4. Awarded honorary doctorate at Cambridge University
        September. *The Black Swan*

1954   January. Purchase of final home in Kilchberg, Switzerland, near Zurich
        September. *Confessions of Felix Krull*
1955   May. Declared honorary citizen of Lübeck
        July. Vacation in Holland interrupted by illness
        August 12. Death in Zurich
        August 16. Burial in Kilchberg cemetery overlooking Lake Zurich

Chapter 1

Introduction

Weimar Republic was Germany's government from
1919 to 1933, the period after WW I until the rise
of the Nazi Germany.

Keywords 2

With the possible exception of Franz Kafka, Thomas Mann (1875–1955) is the best-known German writer of the early twentieth century. Unlike Kafka, however, who was known only to a small circle of admirers until more than a generation after his death, Thomas Mann was famous from the time that he published his first novel in 1901. Mann's cultivated manners and elegant clothing betrayed his patrician origins, and he wrote with the stylistic virtuosity of a nineteenth-century realist, but his works captured the anxious spirit of modern times, full as they were of gender confusion, artistic crisis, physical decline, and moral decay. Had Mann died in 1913, he might have been remembered as a significant writer with a limited range, the author of undisputed masterpieces in *Buddenbrooks* and *Death in Venice* (*Der Tod in Venedig*, 1912), but also of a disappointing second novel, a failed drama, and several half-finished projects. He was well-known in literary circles and popular among general readers, but he was not yet the iconic figure who became known as the living embodiment of German national culture.

History changed all that. When war broke out in August 1914, Thomas Mann – who had never taken much interest in politics – found himself writing patriotic essays. As the war dragged on, Mann wrote page after page of his *Reflections of a Nonpolitical Man*, a work that established his credentials as a leading right-wing intellectual. To everyone's surprise and to the great disappointment of his fellow conservatives, Mann reversed course just four years later to voice his public support for the fledgling democracy of the Weimar Republic. To his own surprise, Mann found himself in exile little more than a decade later, stating sadly in his public break with the Nazi government that he was better suited to be a representative than a martyr. Within a few years, the quintessential German found himself living in California as an American citizen; the "nonpolitical man" was delivering political speeches on a regular basis. Meanwhile, the writing continued and the accolades rained down: novel followed novel, from *The Magic Mountain* through *Joseph and his Brothers* to *Doctor Faustus*;

very imp.

1

the honorary degree that had been revoked by the University of Bonn in 1936 was soon replaced by others from Berkeley, Harvard, Oxford, and Cambridge.

Although celebrated like few other writers, Mann also generated controversy and even inspired hatred. To Bertolt Brecht, Mann was a pompous ass, the embodiment of bourgeois respectability and the antithesis of all that the leather-jacketed, cigar-chewing radical represented. Fellow German exiles resented his fame and fortune. Some suspected him of harboring clandestine Nazi sympathies, while American McCarthyites thought he might be a communist. The posthumous publication of Mann's diaries has kept the controversies swirling into the twenty-first century. They have confirmed the extent of his homosexual desires, shed new and sometimes unflattering light on his role as the patriarch of what was often referred to as his "amazing family," and raised new charges of anti-Semitism.

This volume provides a succinct introduction to Thomas Mann's life and works. The primary focus is on his literary texts, but it also touches on key stages in his personal development and on his evolution as a public intellectual. The book presupposes no prior knowledge of Thomas Mann, but it may serve as a useful reference for those who know his works well. As the book is intended for the general public as well as an academic audience, I have kept quotations and footnotes to a minimum, although I do include suggestions for further reading. Unless otherwise noted, all translations are my own.

Keywords

Thomas Mann experienced more than his share of personal and political upheaval in the course of his long life. In his late teens he moved from his native city of Lübeck to Munich, which in terms of local customs and dialect was about as far as it was possible to move and still be within the German Reich. After more than forty years in Munich he was forced into exile, living first in Switzerland and then for more than a decade in the United States. He returned to Europe in his final years, but not to Germany: he died in Switzerland as an American citizen. Over the years, Mann evolved from a self-absorbed artist with little interest in politics to a prominent public intellectual and a leading voice in the campaign against German National Socialism. This volume will trace Mann's evolution as a writer in response to changing personal circumstances and unfolding historical events, but we begin with an overview of certain aspects of his work and his outlook on life that remained constant in the face of change. For the sake of convenience, I have chosen seven keywords that point to distinct yet interrelated aspects of Mann's fiction and his outlook on the world.

Distinction. In a letter to his brother Heinrich of January 8, 1904, Thomas Mann wrote that his "old prejudice as a Senator's son from Lübeck, an arrogant Hanseatic instinct" had led him to believe "that in comparison with us everything else is inferior." Thomas Mann was raised in a comfortable home with servants in the heart of the city at a time when class distinctions were more rigid than they are today, and he felt throughout his life that he was not cut from common cloth. His father, Thomas Johann Heinrich Mann, was one of the wealthiest men in Lübeck and a high-ranking member of the local government. Years later, Heinrich Mann recalled the extreme deference with which his father was greeted by his fellow citizens. "He was a senator, which at that time did not depend on party affiliation or public elections. It depended solely on the family. Either you were or you were not – and once you attained membership in the Senate, you had the lifelong authority of an absolutist minister."[1] When he died at the age of only fifty-one, the entire city participated in the funeral rites. The death led to the dissolution of the family business and a considerable loss of income, and yet Mann's mother was still able to afford an eight-room apartment when she moved to Munich. "We are not rich," she explained to her children, "but we are well-to-do."

Heinrich and Thomas received monthly allowances from the family estate that were sufficient to support a modest bachelor existence, particularly when they traveled to Italy, where things were cheaper. Unlike Hermann Hesse, who spent years working as a bookstore apprentice, or Franz Kafka, who spent his entire adult life working for an insurance agency, Thomas Mann never held a job. His first novel, *Buddenbrooks*, sold slowly at first, but soon became a bestseller that provided a steady source of income. Mann also married into one of the wealthiest families in Munich. The Mann family lived in a large villa in a fashionable district in Munich; Mann also owned a summer cottage in rural Bavaria and a house on the shores of the Baltic Sea. The commercial success of *The Magic Mountain* (1924) and the Nobel Prize for Literature (1929) brought further fame and fortune. Even in exile, Mann lived well. His novels sold well in English translation and were sometimes featured by the Book of the Month Club. He had the loyal support of Agnes Meyer, a wealthy and politically well-connected Washington insider who eased bureaucratic tensions with American government officials and provided substantial financial support. While many members of the exile community lived in abject poverty, Mann was able to purchase ocean-front property in Southern California, where he wrote in his custom-designed home.

Mann enjoyed the finer things in life. He was a meticulous dresser with a flair for style. One typical photograph of 1929 shows him with his wife Katia in Berlin. Mann is dressed in a double-breasted overcoat and wearing a dapper fedora; he holds a leather briefcase in his left hand with an umbrella hanging from his forearm. His feet are crossed, revealing shiny patent leather shoes and white spats beneath his dark trousers. Although he was only about 5ft 7ins tall, Mann maintained an erect posture and trim figure throughout his life that gave him a more imposing presence than might have been expected for a man of his average stature. Mann liked to travel first class, stay in elegant hotels, and eat at fine restaurants. He also enjoyed his contacts with the rich and famous. In a diary entry of September 12, 1953, for instance, Mann noted with evident satisfaction that he had spent the evening at Charlie Chaplin's estate in Switzerland. "Picked up in Chaplin's car at seven. Short drive through his splendid estate with a gigantic park ... My most pleasant evening in a long time. Delighted by the luxury." In January 1941 Thomas and Katia were the private guests of President and Eleanor Roosevelt at the White House; in April 1953 Mann received a private audience with Pope Pious XII. Throughout his life, then, Mann enjoyed the distinction of one to the manor born; as Tonio Kröger puts it, "after all, we're not gypsies in a green caravan."[2]

Stigma. Despite the advantages of birth, financial success, and public acclaim, Thomas Mann led a difficult life. His sexual desires were a source of constant conflict. As his fiction often suggests and his posthumously published diaries confirmed, Mann was passionately attracted to young men throughout his life. Had he lived in the twenty-first century, he might well have been a practicing homosexual, but the general consensus of his biographers is that he probably never acted on his homosexual desires. There were good reasons to prevent him from coming out: most obviously, homosexuality was illegal and socially unacceptable. Oscar Wilde's sensational trial in 1895 had led to his imprisonment and contributed to his early death; in Germany, Maximilian Harden had exposed a group of homosexuals at Kaiser Wilhelm II's court in a highly publicized scandal that led to lawsuits and public humiliation for the individuals involved, as Mann was well aware. The ambitious young writer was not willing to risk his reputation, and the very sense of distinction that encouraged Mann to cultivate an aura of impeccable taste and middle-class respectability contributed to his sexual reticence. His emphatically heterosexual brother Heinrich suffered from no such shyness, discovering the delights of Lübeck's brothels at an early age and writing lurid fiction that seemed calculated to shock the bourgeoisie. In contrast with Hesse, who interspersed his bouts of drinking and womanizing with soul-searching retreats to the alternative community of Ascona, Switzerland, or Stefan George, who conducted his homosexual toga parties in Munich, Mann lived an outwardly austere and inwardly tormented existence.

Mann's calling as an artist also conflicted with the expectations of his respectable upbringing. His father was outraged when Heinrich quit school and announced his plans to become a writer; in his final will and testament he urged his son's guardians to discourage Heinrich's "literary activity." Although Thomas shared his brother's desire to become a writer, he was also well aware of the dubious social status of the artist in the eyes of the patrician class in Lübeck. As a result, he became something of an artist with a bad conscience, careful to maintain a respectable façade as a well-dressed man with a wife and children, while devoting his creative energy to themes of decadence.

A third stigmatizing factor in Mann's life was his mother's partial Portuguese heritage and his own belief that he was of mixed race, a dark-haired outcast among the Nordic denizens of Lübeck. Thomas Mann's maternal grandfather left Lübeck for Brazil in 1820. There he made his fortune and married the daughter of a Creole plantation owner of Portuguese descent. Mann's mother Julia was sent back to Lübeck at the age of seven after her mother died, and she arrived to a strange new world of unknown relatives, speaking at first only Portuguese. Julia often told her children stories about her childhood in the tropics, growing up as the privileged daughter of a plantation owner surrounded by African slaves and the Brazilian jungles. This family history contributed to Mann's sense of being unlike his fellow youths in Lübeck and made him sensitive at an early age to others who, like himself, seemed marked by sexual "deviance" or racial difference; he had a particularly complicated relationship with German Jews.

Representation. When Mann arrived in the United States on February 21, 1938, a reporter for the *New York Times* asked him "whether he found his exile a difficult burden." Mann admitted that it was difficult, but given the "poisoned atmosphere in Germany," it was just as well to be away. And yet, he continued, he was in a certain sense not away at all: "Where I am, there is Germany. I carry German culture in me." Mann's famous declaration can be read in two ways, either as a modest, matter-of-fact statement that he was so steeped in German culture that it made no difference where he was in any given moment, or as a grandiose claim to be the living embodiment of the German nation. Seen in the larger context of his career, it becomes evident that Mann meant these words in both senses, referring simultaneously to his personal embeddedness in one cultural tradition and his conviction that his own struggles and preoccupations were representative of the nation as a whole. Mann always strove for more than personal success; he also wanted to be Germany's most representative writer. In later years, Mann often intervened directly in political affairs, but he was convinced throughout his career that he was a cultural seismograph – an artist who was intuitively in touch with the spirit of the age and spoke as the voice of the nation, even in literary works that seemed on the surface to have little or nothing to do with current events.

The notion of the writer as a representative of the people has multiple roots in German culture. Readers outside Germany may not realize the high social status of writers and the important role they play in political debates. For instance, the events that led to German Reunification in 1989–90 were accompanied by an impassioned debate among artists and intellectuals about the nature of the German nation in the light of its troubled past. Günter Grass, one of the leading opponents to Reunification at the time, made headlines again in 2006 when he admitted that he had been a member of the Waffen-SS – after spending decades castigating others who had been less than entirely honest about their involvement in the Nazi past. The revelations became the focus of a media frenzy in Germany not only because they revealed what some felt was evidence of personal hypocrisy, but also because of Grass' immense cultural prestige as a Nobel Laureate and Germany's most recognizable postwar writer. The individual became a public symbol for Germany's ongoing attempt to come to terms with the past.

Thomas Mann played a similarly representative role in earlier twentieth-century German culture, continuing what was already then a long tradition. Eighteenth-century aristocrats led what Jürgen Habermas has described as a representative existence.[3] Unlike members of the modern middle class, who tend to identify with their professions and define themselves by what they have learned to do, aristocrats display who they are as a result of the privilege of birth. As the son of a quasi-aristocratic member of Lübeck's oligarchy, Mann inherited vestiges of this ethos: "I do have a certain princely talent for representation, if I am more or less in good form," wrote Thomas with smug satisfaction to Heinrich on February 27, 1904, after his first appearance in the glittering salon of his future in-laws in Munich. The notion of the writer as sounding board of the social conscience also has roots in post-revolutionary romanticism. As the authority of the Church and monarchy was challenged, poets tried to find meaning in a world turned upside down, a process that was by nature fraught with difficulty. Romantic writers alternated between moments of exhilaration and despair, between the proud conviction that they were the new, if "unacknowledged legislators of the world," as Percy Bysshe Shelley put it, and the fear that they were adrift and "alone, alone on a wide wide sea," to quote Samuel T. Coleridge's ancient mariner. As a writer who reflected throughout his career on the problematic relationship between the artist and society, Thomas Mann was a direct heir to the aesthetics of German romanticism. Mann's conviction that he was a representative of the German people has still a third, more sinister connection to the *völkisch* ideology of late nineteenth- and early twentieth-century Germany. Writers such as Paul de Lagarde, Julius Lahnbehn, and Arthur Moeller van den Bruck conceived of the nation not as a group of citizens with a common commitment to the principles of democracy, but as a people (*Volk*) bound together by blood relations, rooted in the ancestral soil, and imbued with a common spirit. The writer served as the mystical conduit for the general will, the spiritual medium for the collective unconsciousness. Mann was deeply influenced as a young man by such writers, and even when he had made his decisive break away from what Fritz Stern has called "the politics of cultural despair,"[4] he insisted that he should not be viewed as "the good German" who condemned Germany's descent into barbarism from the perspective of a detached observer. "Nothing that I was able to tell you or suggest about Germany came from an alien, cool, detached intellectual perspective," wrote Mann in 1945 toward the end of his speech to an American public on the topic of "Germany and the Germans." "I have it all in me, I have experienced it all myself."

Confession. In May 1945, Thomas Mann's son Golo saw his father walking back across the lawn of their property in Pacific Palisades, California, from the direction of an incinerator used to burn unwanted documents. A look into the oven revealed that Mann had just burned a large amount of paper, although exactly what he had destroyed remained unclear until the publication of his diaries many years later. "Carried out an old resolution to destroy old diaries," we read in his entry of May 21, 1945. "Burned them in the incinerator outside." This was not the first time that Mann had destroyed all-too-private documents. Already in 1896 Mann confessed in a letter of February 17 to his boyhood friend Otto Grautoff that he had burned his diaries. "Why? Because I found them annoying ... And what if I suddenly died? It would be embarrassing and unpleasant to have left behind such a large quantity of secret – *very* secret – writing." During the first months of exile in 1933, Mann was terrified that the diaries that he had left in Munich might fall into the wrong hands; fortunately, Golo managed to smuggle them across the border unread. Mann wrote in his diaries only when he was alone and undisturbed, and no one, including his wife, was allowed to read them. He nevertheless decided in 1950 that he would preserve the diaries that he had begun in 1933, although he sealed them with the instruction that they were not to be opened until twenty or twenty-five years after his death: "Let the world know me," he noted on October 13, 1950, "but only when everyone is dead."

Mann's fluctuation between a need to confess and an impulse to conceal extended to other aspects of his life and works. He once referred to *Doctor Faustus* as a "radical confession," but the same could be said of *Tonio Kröger* or *Death in Venice*, both of which draw directly on Mann's own experience. Mann also felt free to exploit the private lives of family and friends for his fiction: he outraged his uncle by portraying him as the dissolute Christian Buddenbrook; he worked some of his own love letters to his future wife into *Royal Highness* (*Königliche Hoheit*, 1909); and he transcribed verbatim the description of his sister Carla's suicide into *Doctor Faustus*. Mann's essays about other writers are often also indirect self-portraits. Even the homosexuality that he was at such pains to conceal was an open secret to his wife and his daughter Erika, and homoeroticism abounds in his literary works – hence his biographer Anthony Heilbut has aptly termed Thomas Mann "the poet of a half-open closet."[5]

Mann's confessional impulse is deeply rooted in the Christian tradition that was of particular importance to the eighteenth-century German Pietist movement. Pietists rejected what they felt had become the stultifying rituals of the official Protestant Church and infused religious experience with enthusiasm and introspection. Believers were encouraged to look within themselves and to record their spiritual progress from sin to salvation in autobiographical narratives. Another source of Mann's tendency toward the autobiographical in his writing lay in his desire to emulate Goethe, who had famously termed his own literary productions "fragments of a great confession" in his autobiography, *Poetry and Truth* (*Dichtung und Wahrheit*). If Mann were to become modern Germany's most representative writer, then he had to become the Goethe of his century. Yet the very desire to imitate Goethe suggests that there is an element of dissimulation or role playing combined with the soul-baring impulse of the confession. Mann's *Confessions of Felix Krull* continues the literary tradition of the fictional autobiography, and yet Mann's protagonist is without psychological depth and as malleable as a chameleon. Like Goethe, whose stylistic virtuosity allowed him to write seemingly naïve German folksongs, highly stylized "Roman" elegies, and pseudo-Persian poetry, Mann was a master of deception as well as confession. Mann's correspondence, for instance, reveals diplomatic skills that contrast markedly with the unvarnished revelations of his intimate diaries. His many letters to his American benefactress Agnes Meyer are full of flattery to the point of obsequiousness, although the relationship was often tense. When Golo told his father that Mrs. Meyer suspected that Mann actually despised her, he was impressed: "Since my letters are full of devotion, admiration, thankfulness, concern, and even gallantry, that is a very intelligent observation" (diary entry of February 14, 1944).

Entertainment. Late in life, Mann reacted angrily to the charge that his style was "ponderous" or "pompous." "None of these attributes are in the least pertinent, believe me!" he wrote (in English) to Kenneth Oliver in a letter of May 4, 1951. "Complete lucidity, musicality, and a serenity that lightens what might otherwise be heavy – this is what my prose has always tried to achieve. In addition to that, I admit, there is a playful tendency towards irony and subtle parody upon tradition." Despite these denials, Mann is still frequently associated with Teutonic humorlessness, and the diaries reveal an often moody, at times even clinically depressed, individual. Yet Mann was not always full of gloom and doom. "He could be very funny indeed," Katia recalled after his death,[6] even if his sense of humor was sometimes in questionable taste by today's standards. His younger brother Viktor recalled that Mann had his family and friends in stitches when he appeared for a costume party in formal evening dress but wearing the mask of an idiot. Mann reduced the group to gasps of hilarity by absent-mindedly scratching his deformed nose with a hand encased in an elegant lace glove, a gesture that Viktor suspected – probably correctly – Mann had practiced in front of a mirror before entering the room.

Mann was an entertainer. Throughout his career he gave public readings of his fiction, usually to packed houses, and he was disappointed if an audience seemed unresponsive or failed to call him back for several curtain calls. He was also keen to stress the comic elements in his fiction. "I wish I knew why I give the impression of Olympian pretentiousness!" he complained somewhat disingenuously in a letter of July 17, 1944 to Agnes Meyer. "I really just want to make people laugh and otherwise I try to be the personification of modesty." Mann's writing can indeed be funny. It contains a number of broadly comic scenes, such as the side-splitting depiction of unruly students tormenting their hapless teachers in *Buddenbrooks* and Felix Krull's performance of epilepsy in front of the draft board, as well as subtler elements of irony and parody throughout his work. Unlike James Joyce or the German Expressionists, Mann never wrote experimental prose. His sentences may be long and his syntax complex, but he is never grammatically incorrect. His works have layers of symbolic density and display philosophical profundity, but they can always be read for the plot as well.

"I want to appeal to stupid readers too," Mann once wrote half-seriously to Hermann Hesse (letter of April 1, 1910), referring to his appropriation of Richard Wagner's "double optic," that is, music or prose that appeals simultaneously to high-brow intellectuals and the general reading public. There are a number of reasons for Mann's adoption of this strategy. One lies in his personal temperament, his desire to at least appear reasonable and respectable in his prose style as well as his personal appearance. Another may be found in Mann's need to earn a living from his prose. He had a wife and six children to support, after all, and he was also quite generous in his contributions to other family members, friends, and public causes. Finally, Mann took seriously the classical dictum that the poet is to delight as well as instruct; he was also convinced that the true virtuoso should be able to make the most difficult tasks look easy. Mann's goal, in short, was to treat "heavy" themes lightly, to cloak modernist prose in the garb of nineteenth-century realism, to tell sad stories that make people laugh.

Discipline. Together with the penchant for introspection that Mann may have inherited from his Protestant ancestors was a daily commitment to hard work. Or perhaps he was still trying to please the father who had died when he was only fifteen. In a speech delivered in Lübeck two months before his death, Mann wished that his father could have been present to see his son proclaimed an honorary citizen of the city. "I can say this much: his image has stood behind everything I have done, and I have always regretted that I gave him so little cause for hope when he was alive that I would ever achieve any sort of respectability."[7] If he could not be a successful businessman or senator, at least he could work like one, and he did. Klaus Mann has left a memorable description of his father's workday: between the hours of nine and twelve each morning the children understood from an early age that their father was not to be disturbed: "To enter his studio while he is mysteriously occupied there would be as blasphemous as to invade the temple when a secret ceremonial is taking place."[8] Mann's children called him "The Magician" (*Der Zauberer*), a nickname that derived from an outfit he once wore to a costume party, but that captured the aura of mystery that shrouded his morning work hours. Mann evidently enjoyed the name, as he often signed letters to his children with a simple "Z."

Mann wrote slowly but kept most of what he wrote. He must have had a clear conception of the entire work before writing, because he would sometimes send early chapters of a novel to the typesetter before having written the conclusion. He wrote by hand on large sheets of paper in a cramped handwriting that is difficult to decipher. Writing was a sober affair, reserved for the morning hours, and never stimulated by alcohol or other drugs, although he did smoke cigarettes and cigars throughout his life. Afternoons were reserved for the noon meal, a long walk with his dog, reading and correspondence, with the assistance of a secretary or Katia in later years – Katia learned how to type so that she could assist her husband and often wrote letters in his name – and a nap. As Klaus recalled, the magician's naptime was as sacrosanct as his work time, and the children knew that their father was not to be disturbed. Evenings were often an opportunity for socializing with friends or attending performances of classical music, the theater, or the opera; Mann also enjoyed the movies and playing records of classical music on his gramophone at home. If all went well, Mann was up and writing in his office the next morning.

Of course things did not always go well: even in the best of times, Mann became sick, went on lecture tours, or came up against creative impasses; later years brought the burdens of fame, including political essays, public perform-ances, and endless correspondence, the disruption of exile, and the exhaustion of old age. The myth that Mann punched the clock at nine and produced a steady stream of prose until twelve each day is just that, a myth. Writing was difficult for Mann. In a bon mot that he includes in the novella *Tristan*, Mann defines the writer as someone who finds it more difficult than others to write, or, as he put it in a letter to Heinrich of December 7, 1908, "it is curious that all the best work on the brink of exhaustion" – a phrase that found its way into *Death in Venice* a few years later. Mann accepted the inevitability of death, but he was terrified by the thought that he might get to the point where he could no longer write. During the first weeks of exile when Mann was interrupted in his work on the Joseph novels, his diary entries swell to page-long essays, suggesting that his need to write something, anything each day had found an alternative outlet. Eventually, however, he did manage to complete *Joseph and his Brothers*, a four-volume opus that moved with him from his comfortable villa in Munich to the years of exile in the United States, just as he completed *Doctor Faustus* after recovering from a major operation for lung cancer. Mann was justifiably proud of his ability to complete such projects under difficult circumstances. On January 4, 1943, for instance, he noted that he had com-pleted the Joseph novels after nearly two decades: "I was excited and sad. But it is finished, one way or the other. I see it much more as a monument to my life than to art, a monument to *persistence.*"

Catastrophe. The belated desire to please his father and the Protestant work-ethic may have motivated Mann's daily dedication to his work, but writing was also a form of sexual sublimation, a way to keep the forces at bay that threatened to destroy the fragile edifice of his outwardly respect-able life. "It is the idea of visitation (*Heimsuchung*) by drunken, ruinous, and destructive powers invading a life of composure," writes Mann of Joseph when tempted by Potiphar's wife, but also of himself.[9] In an early letter, Mann referred half-ironically to his sexual urges as "the dogs in the basement," wild animals always threatening to break loose (to Otto Grautoff, February 17, 1906). Like Hans Castorp, the protagonist of *The Magic Mountain*, Mann was confronted by death at an early age and sometimes flirted with the thought of his own premature demise. In a letter to Heinrich of February 28, 1901, Mann suggested half-seriously that he wished for "a good case of typhus with a satisfying outcome," and although he reassured Heinrich in his next letter that he would not do "anything stupid" for the time being, he was surrounded by others who did: both of his sisters committed suicide, as did his son Klaus.

Mann's youngest son Michael also succumbed to a probably suicidal combination of barbiturates and alcohol in 1977. Mann was plagued by tooth pain and intestinal discomfort throughout his life and also suffered from anxiety attacks and insomnia.

Mann's sense that catastrophe could strike his personal life at any moment was exacerbated by the political events that he witnessed, including Germany's defeat in the First World War, the unchecked inflation of the early 1920s, the Depression, and, above all, the rise and fall of the Third Reich. Mann likened German fascism to an upwelling of destructive forces lying latent in the German soul, an unchaining of Cerberus from the gates of hell. Mann's effort to maintain control of his life in exile was both a personal necessity and a political statement: Germany should not have let itself go, should not have opened the gates to the forces of destruction lying latent in its soul. Mann managed to keep those "dogs in the basement," but he lived a life of what he termed an "austere happiness" at best,[10] longing for sexual satisfaction that he would never experience, struggling to remain productive in the face of physical discomfort and emotional turmoil, and haunted by the constant fear that the forces of chaos could shatter the delicate equilibrium of his world.

Chapter 2

Origins, influences, and early mastery

Childhood and early influences

Thomas Mann was born in Lübeck on the morning of June 6, 1875. At that time Lübeck was a moderately sized city of approximately 35,000 inhabitants, but it had known greater days in the past. During the late Middle Ages, Lübeck had been the capital of the Hanseatic League, a far-flung trade network extending across northern Europe from St. Petersburg to the Netherlands. Wealth from the trade in grain, furs, timber, amber, and wool flowed into the coffers of the Lübeck merchants and financed the construction of the imposing city gates, the striking town hall, and the great brick Gothic cathedral of St. Mary, where Thomas Mann was baptized. In the course of the fifteenth century, however, the Hanseatic League began to unravel; the subsequent depredations of the Thirty Years War and the Napoleonic occupation accelerated the decline of what had once been one of Germany's wealthiest cities. Modest growth resumed in the course of the nineteenth century, but industrialization and the expansion of transatlantic trade directed shipping away from Lübeck and toward the boom-ing harbor of Hamburg. Perhaps because of its relative insignificance, Lübeck was spared total devastation in the Allied bombing campaigns of the Second World War, and by the time of Mann's death in 1955, it had completed its transformation from the "Queen of the Hansa" to the picturesque town that continues to attract tourists today.

Mann's early horizons were both narrow and broad. As an adult, Mann went on extensive lecture tours in Europe and North America, sailed back and forth across the Atlantic long before flights made international travel routine, and spent more than thirty years in exile. By the time of his eighteenth birthday, in contrast, Mann had seen little more than his hometown. To be from Lübeck meant to be surrounded by the local dialect of Low German (*Plattdeutsch*), which

Mann could understand and imitate in his works, even if he spoke standard German (*Hochdeutsch*) at home and in school. Being from Lübeck also meant living in the crowded streets of a harbor town, breathing the cool, damp air of northern Europe with endless summer days and correspondingly long winter nights, and taking the occasional family vacation to nearby Travemünde, a resort on the shore of the Baltic Sea. Yet because of its commercial ties to Russia, Scandinavia, and Great Britain, Lübeck had a cosmopolitan openness that belied its provinciality. The characters in the partially autobiographical *Buddenbrooks* smoke Russian cigarettes and conduct business in England, speak Danish and French as well as Low German, travel to places such as Vienna and Paris, and send their sons to work in Norway and London. Mann's father was born in Lübeck, but his father's mother was Swiss and his mother's mother was a Portuguese Creole living in Brazil.

Further complicating the mixture of provincialism and cosmopolitanism in Lübeck were tensions that arose between the old Hanseatic city-state and the new Prussian-centered nation-state. Germany's first political unification took place only four years before Mann's birth, but regional loyalties remained strong. From an economic standpoint, Lübeck could not compete with Berlin, but, as Mann argued in his *Reflections of a Nonpolitical Man*, there were certain advantages to growing up where he did. Berlin was an industrial city of the imperial age that had the bare-knuckled bravado of a modern metropolis, but it lacked the introspective creativity associated with the proverbial "land of poets and thinkers" (*das Land der Dichter und Denker*). Lübeck retained the quieter virtues of an earlier age, where patricians took care of political business and citizens of a certain social status could enjoy the classical virtue of self-cultivation (*Bildung*). In the essay "Lübeck as a Spiritual Form of Life" ("Lübeck als geistige Lebensform," 1926), however, Mann suggested that the sense of unbroken continuity with the past in Lübeck also had something uncanny, mysterious, and even demonic about it. Mann would attribute these characteristics to the fictional city of Kaisersaschern in *Doctor Faustus*, which he describes as a place where time stood still and one had the sense that at any moment mass hysteria might break out in a throwback from modern civilization into medieval madness.

By his own admission, Thomas Mann was a terrible student. He was held back to repeat a grade three times, and although he finally did graduate with a low-level degree (*mittlere Reife*), he never took the prestigious *Abitur*, the comprehensive examination that qualifies German students for university attendance. Lack of intelligence was not to blame. Mann found his teachers arrogant and stupid, and the stress on military uniforms and physical prowess distasteful. One of his former fellow students recalled that Mann practiced a kind of passive resistance in his physical education class, symbolically touching the gymnastic apparatus with his fingertips with a look of withering disdain. The aloof posture of the privileged senator's son masked a shyness that further distanced him from teachers he could not respect and students who either repulsed him with their coarse vitality or aroused clandestine homosexual desires. By the time that he graduated at the age of nineteen – others attained the same degree at sixteen – Mann had long since given up on the school, and the school had given up on him.

As a result, Mann became a lifelong autodidact. His earliest reading included Greek and Roman mythology, the *Iliad*, and a book about the Egyptian pyramids; as he later recalled, he was never interested in adventure novels such as *The Last of the Mohicans* that were popular among his peers. The works of German and other European authors soon followed. Mann received an edition of Friedrich Schiller's works for Christmas in 1889, which marked the beginning of a lifelong love for the poet and dramatist. Mann was not interested in Schiller as the passionate proponent of human rights, but rather as a sensitive and determined artist. "The king wept" is the line that captures Tonio Kröger's imagination, not the Marquis von Posa's more famous plea for freedom of thought. In *Difficult Hour* (*Schwere Stunde*, 1905), Mann will identify with Schiller as a disciplined writer who created in the face of mental and physical anguish, as opposed to those such as Goethe, and, implicitly, his brother Heinrich, who seemed to write with effortless ease. Mann was also familiar with Goethe at an early age – he lists Faust and Mephistopheles among his favorite characters in an early essay[1] – but the intense identification with Goethe would come later. Other early influences included late nineteenth-century German realists, in particular the poetry and prose of the north German Theodor Storm and the social novels of Theodor Fontane. Heinrich Heine was another favorite. Mann's mother sang German *Lieder* that included poetry by Heine and his fellow romantic Joseph Freiherr von Eichendorff set to the music of Robert Schumann. Mann was also influenced by the poetry of August von Platen, a melancholy aristocrat who wrote formally chiseled poems centering on themes of beauty, death, and homoeroticism, and the Austrian critic Hermann Bahr, who rejected socially engaged naturalist art in favor of symbolism and aestheticism.

Thomas' older brother Heinrich occupies a special place in his early career and subsequent development. The openly rebellious Heinrich served as both role-model and rival for young Thomas. Heinrich introduced Thomas to many of his early intellectual and literary influences, and provided an example of a life devoted to art that contrasted with his father's business world. Heinrich Mann's first novel, *In a Family* (*In einer Familie*), published with his mother's financial support in 1893, brings together several themes that resonate throughout Thomas Mann's fiction as well: his mother's exotic origins in Brazil, the intoxicating power of Wagner's music, the dangers of female sexuality, and the forbidden lure of incest. Thomas and Heinrich were contributing editors for a right-wing, anti-Semitic journal in 1895 – an episode that both carefully repressed in later years – and they lived together for extended periods in Italy. Increasingly, however, artistic, political, and temperamental differences drove them apart. Thomas found his brother's fiction crassly sensationalistic, his increasingly liberal politics alienating, and his choice of women unacceptable. Already as adolescents the two brothers spent an entire year refusing to talk to one another even though they shared the same room; that silence would stretch for nearly a decade in a bitter feud sparked by their contrasting opinions regarding Germany's entry into the First World War. As a result, Heinrich's influence was both positive and negative; he was both a source of identification and a bad example to be rejected. As Thomas Buddenbrook will say in a moment of uncontrolled rage to his brother Christian, "I have become what I am because I did not want to become like you!"[2]

Mann read widely in other European literatures as well, although he was the first to admit that he had no talent for foreign languages. Mann retained some of his schoolboy Latin, had basic conversational French, a smattering of Italian, and eventually learned a fairly fluent, if heavily accented English, but he read most non-German authors in translation. As he insisted in an essay on "Cosmopolitanism" in 1925, however, there is not only nothing wrong with reading in translation – "who can read Hungarian anyway?" – but also those who think they are reading undiluted German literature when they read an author such as Goethe are mistaken: there are so many foreign influences in his works that it is deeply European, not narrowly German. Mann admired Dante's *Divine Comedy*, Cervantes' *Don Quixote*, Dickens, and Shakespeare, but his deepest love was for Scandinavian and Russian literature. He knew Hans Christian Andersen's fairy tales from childhood, acted in a performance of Ibsen's *Wild Duck* in Munich, and admired the prose of Herman Bang, Jens Peter Jacobsen, and the Norwegian Knut Hamsun, although Mann would later disapprove of his support for German fascism. Tolstoy's Homeric grandeur and Dostoevsky's psychologically tormented heroes exerted a lifelong appeal, but Mann also appreciated such Russian authors as Pushkin, Gogol, Lermontov, and Chekov. "Of course I am not a Bolshevik," Mann wrote to his friend Julius Bab on September 5, 1920, "(although I am still a good Russian, just as I always was)."

In the *Reflections of a Nonpolitical Man*, Mann singled out Richard Wagner, Friedrich Nietzsche, and Arthur Schopenhauer as his three most significant intellectual influences. In the days before records and radios, music had to be heard live, and Mann had the good fortune to have regular access to an inexpensive seat at the Lübeck opera. There he was enraptured by a performance of *Lohengrin*, beginning a lifelong love affair – when Mann returned to Lübeck a few months before his death, the city honored him by playing music from *Lohengrin*, and eye-witnesses noted that Mann was visibly moved. Wagner's music was intoxicating for Mann, a source of sensual pleasure that he sought out almost like a drug or sex. As noted earlier, Mann also admired Wagner's ability to appeal to a wide range of listeners, just as Mann hoped to appeal to average readers as well as intellectuals. For this very reason, however, Mann was also suspicious of Wagner, whose music he described as "monumental dilettantism" in an essay of 1933,[3] overwrought kitsch that pandered to the masses. That those masses of Wagner fans also included Adolf Hitler was particularly embarrassing, and there were many times when Mann rejected his music as more bombastic than seductive. Mann did not criticize Wagner publicly for his virulent anti-Semitism, however, although he did comment privately on his distaste for the figure of Beckmesser in *Die Meistersinger*, whom Mann saw as a coded Jewish stereotype (diary entry of May 26, 1954).

Mann's enthusiasm for Wagner was widespread among intellectuals of his generation, as was the interest in Nietzsche. As Steven E. Aschheim has shown in his study of *The Nietzsche Legacy in Germany*, Nietzsche was embraced by a bewildering range of followers: avant-garde artists and reactionary politicians, warmongers and vegetarians, atheists and Christians. For many, including Heinrich Mann, Nietzsche inspired a cult of the Renaissance that stressed ruthless vitality against the alleged decadence of bourgeois society. As an artist and intellectual with patrician roots, Thomas Mann also felt distinguished from the common herd, as Nietzsche called it, but his sense of superiority was accompanied by a touch of guilt and a wish that he could share the apparent simplicity of the average citizen's daily routine. He therefore moved away from Heinrich's confrontational art and lifestyle toward what he described in the *Reflections* as "erotic irony": an erotic attraction to "life" (usually, if clandestinely, in the form of handsome young men) combined with the ironic detachment of the artist. Mann's increasing skepticism toward Wagner was also inspired by Nietzsche, who had begun his career as an ardent Wagnerian and ended it as Wagner's arch enemy. Mann shared with Nietzsche a critical perspective on the militant nationalism and aggressive imperialism of Germany under Bismarck and his successors, and his works often reflect Nietzsche's misogyny as well.

Both Wagner and Nietzsche were influenced by Schopenhauer, who had published his magnum opus, *The World as Will and Representation* (1819), at the astonishingly early age of twenty-one. Immanuel Kant had claimed in his *Critique of Pure Reason* (1781) that we can never know reality directly (what he termed *das Ding an sich*, or, the thing itself), but only reality as it is filtered through the categories that structure our perception. For Johann Gottlieb Fichte, Kant's philosophy was a breath of fresh air that liberated the human spirit from the constraints of empirical reality, but the writer Heinrich von Kleist was thrown into a crisis by his reading of Kant, as he feared that we could never know whether our perception of the world was accurate or not. Schopenhauer boldly declared that he did know what the *Ding an sich* was: it was what he termed the *will*, an amoral life-force that holds us all in its thrall. In contrast with the philosophies of Hegel and Marx, both of whom believed in human progress – the former toward the absolute spirit, the latter toward the material triumph of the proletariat – Schopenhauer's philosophy was radically anti-historical and deeply pessimistic. As embodied beings, we are all shackled to the blind desire of the will; the best we can do is to achieve momentary detachment from its tyranny in the contemplation of art. For a writer such as Thomas Mann, who struggled on a daily basis with his unruly sexual urges, the appeal of Schopenhauer's philosophy is obvious. As he matured into a public intellectual, Mann worked hard to do and say the right thing, to support democracy and to condemn tyranny, but as an artist he remained influenced by Schopenhauer and Nietzsche, infused with the grim conviction that the belief in rationality and progress is merely a life-sustaining illusions against the bedrock of suffering and blind desire.

[handwritten annotation: the opposite of Buddhism. In Buddhism the]

First novellas

With the exception of a single drama and an autobiographical poem written shortly after the First World War, Mann is known as a writer of prose fiction. In the beginning, however, he aspired to be a poet and dramatist. In his earliest extant letter, the fourteen-year-old signed his name as "Th. Mann. Lyric-dramatic poet" (October 14, 1889). Nothing remains of Mann's earliest attempts at drama, but there are a few snippets of adolescent poetry that tend toward a sort of heartfelt sentimentality that he soon learned to avoid. Telling for his ambition even at this early age is a poem in which he fantasizes about future fame. Mann's earliest published works appeared in a student journal that he edited with his friend Otto Grautoff in the summer of 1893, Mann's last in Lübeck. These included a few poems, the short essay on Heine, and, most notably, the two-page prose fragment "Vision." In it a man is captivated by the image of a crystal goblet partially filled with wine held by the hand of his former lover. The identity of the individuals and the precise nature of their relationship is left vague, surrounded in the clouds of smoke that drift from the man's cigarette in a visionary experience that hovers between dream and memory. The mood of the piece reflects Mann's early indebtedness to the anti-naturalist aesthetics of Hermann Bahr and other *fin-de-siècle* writers, although within the fragment are also precisely described details of the sort that would become the hallmark of Mann's mature prose.

Mann's first story to be published in a literary journal was written at his desk while "working" as an unpaid volunteer at a fire insurance company during his first months in Munich in 1894. *Fallen (Gefallen)* is constructed as a framed narrative of the sort employed by Guy de Maupassant, Ivan Turgenev, Theodor Storm, and Anton Chekov, all of whom Mann admired. A man tells a group of his friends what turns out to be an autobiographical story of a young man who falls in love with a seemingly innocent woman, only to discover that she is a prostitute. The title initially awakens expectations of two contrasting literary precedents: either the eighteenth-century motif of the rake who preys on innocent girls, as in Faust's seduction of Gretchen in Goethe's drama, or the nineteenth-century tale of the prostitute with a heart of gold (Verdi's *La Traviata*, *The Fallen Woman*). Mann's tale takes a different, more cynical tack: when the young man surprises his lover eating breakfast with an older man and notices a stack of bills next to the bed, she frankly admits that she entertains men for money and that, while she is willing to play the ingénue on stage, reality leaves her no room for sentimentality. The novella is noteworthy both for its hostility toward women and for its portrayal of weak, insecure men. The narrator tells his tale to disabuse one of his companions of his misguided sympathy for the emancipation of women. Do not be deceived, he cautions, women are not to be trusted. "The woman who falls for love today will fall for money tomorrow." Combined with the inherent duplicity of women is their ability to inflict pain on men. The revelation of his lover's infidelity shatters the confidence of the young man, provoking a combination of self-pity and impotent rage that will recur repeatedly in Mann's early fiction.

Thomas Mann was delighted to receive a flattering letter from the then-famous author Richard Dehmel, who encouraged Mann to send him more of his work for publication in his new journal, *Pan*; even Heinrich condescended to praise his brother's novella as "a nice little indication of talent." Mann's career nevertheless got off to a slow start over the next few years, although it should be remembered that he was only nineteen when he wrote *Fallen*. He soon quit his position at the insurance company, became involved in the artistic scene in Schwabing, Munich, audited a few classes at the university, and, in the summer of 1895, embarked with Heinrich on the first of several extensive trips to Italy. Here Mann continued to write short prose works, a few of which were published, but it was not until 1897 that he published *Little Herr*

Friedemann (*Der kleine Herr Friedemann*), the novella that he considered his artistic breakthrough and that opened the door to lasting fame. On May 23, 1896 Mann had written to Grautoff about a "new, completely psychopathic novella," and two weeks later he told Grautoff that since writing *Little Herr Friedemann* he had "suddenly found the discreet forms and masks that allow me to circulate in public with my experiences ... it is as if some sort of chains had fallen away from me ... as if only now I have been granted the means to express myself, to communicate myself."

"The nurse was to blame." With this lapidary sentence *Little Herr Friedemann* begins. Frau Consul Friedemann returns from an outing with her three young daughters to find her maid in a drunken stupor next to the badly injured baby that she carelessly allowed to fall off the changing table. At first glance we seem to be in the world of German naturalism, which was in vogue in the 1890s. In 1889, Gerhardt Hauptmann had caused a scandal with his first drama, *Before Sunrise* (*Vor Sonnenaufgang*), a sensational portrait of chronic alcoholism in a family of Silesian peasants; in 1893, his incendiary *The Weavers* (*Die Weber*) focused on workers forced into abject poverty by the advent of modern technology. Those expecting socially engaged art from either of the Mann brothers at this stage of their careers would be mistaken, however. Heinrich Mann reacted angrily against the "socialist spirit" of *The Weavers* when he attended the premiere in Berlin, which he associated at that time with Jewishness: "I sat the whole time in silent amazement, and if that evening failed to make me an anti-Semite, then I clearly have no talent for it."[4]

A decade later Heinrich had already moved from right to left in the political spectrum, but his brother had not: "I have no interest in political freedom," wrote Thomas to Heinrich on February 27, 1904 in response to what he termed his brother's "strangely interesting" if "improbable" turn toward liberalism. One year earlier Thomas Mann had published *The Hungry Ones* (*Die Hungernden*), in which a stylishly dressed young man leaves an opera performance in a huff because he has seen his beloved flirting with another man. On the street he encounters a man in rags who observes him with a mixture of envy and scorn, but the young man feels misunderstood: "We are brothers, after all," he exclaims – the one, a homeless beggar cast out from society, the other, an artist who remains tragically detached from the life and love that he ardently desires. The point of the novella is not to right social wrongs, however, but to illustrate the suffering of the self-pitying artist.

Already in *Little Herr Friedemann*, Mann's focus is psychological and pathological, not sociological. As a result of his fall, little Johannes Friedemann grows up stunted and misshapen. When a brief infatuation for a schoolgirl ends in ridicule, he resigns himself to a solitary existence. He takes a job with a local company and devotes his free time to the arts: reading current fiction, attending the opera, and playing his violin. All seems under control until a new military commandant for the district comes to town with his wife, Gerda von Rinnlingen. Friedemann observes her at the opera, visits her at her home, and gradually becomes obsessed with her. In the end she invites him to a party. They walk out into the garden, where he falls to his knees, buries his head in her lap, and stammers a few words. She regards him coldly for a moment and then flings his misshapen body to the ground. He crawls to the bank of a nearby river, collapses, and drowns. After a moment the insects resume the quiet chirping that mingles with the muted laughter of the remaining guests.

Little Herr Friedemann presents one of Mann's central themes and recurring nightmares: the visitation of destructive forces that shatter a life based on the renunciation of desire. To the casual reader, the story would seem to have nothing to do with its author. Those in the know will find repeated autobiographical clues in *Little Herr Friedemann*, however, that suggest Mann's presence behind his fictional mask: Friedemann lives in a medium-sized commercial city reminiscent of Lübeck; his deceased father was Consul to the Netherlands, a title also held by Mann's father. Friedemann's penchant for stylish clothing, violin playing, and Wagnerian opera are all Mann's own, as is his struggle to maintain control over the forces that threaten to destroy him.

The combination of veiled confession and clinical detachment from his fictional characters is typical of Mann's early fiction. On the one hand, he portrays a series of grotesque figures noteworthy for their strange names and bizarre characters. *Tobias Mindernickel* (1897) is an unflinching portrait of a lonely man's sadistic treatment of his beloved dog: he stabs it in a furious outburst and then cuddles it as it bleeds to death. Lobgott Piepsam, the protagonist of *The Path to the Cemetery* (*Der Weg zum Friedhof*, 1900), works himself into an apoplectic rage before he is carted off to an insane asylum. *Little Louise* (*Luischen*, 1897) is the story of a grotesquely fat lawyer who collapses and dies while dancing in a little pink dress. On the other hand, Mann's early fiction contains barely disguised self-portraits, most obviously in *The Joker* (*Der Bajazzo*, 1897), about a young man from a family of businessmen in northern Germany who inherits enough money to lead a life of desultory travel and dilettantish aestheticism. The major difference between Mann and his fictional creations is that they lose control and he does not. Mann's early novellas allowed him to project aspects of himself onto more or less distorted fictional self-portraits, but the resulting works are remarkable for their psychological precision and lack of sentimentality. Not without reason, Mann was often accused of being a cold, unfeeling writer, a reputation that he would later struggle to refute.

While Mann's fiction may have been inspired by his conflicted attitude toward his chosen profession and sexual orientation, it touched a nerve with the general public that elevated it above the merely autobiographical. Three themes in particular resonated with the spirit of the age: the sense of masculinity in crisis, the related fear and loathing of women, and a fascination with the foreign that hovered between exoticism and xenophobia. Within a few years Thomas Mann had gone from being the privileged son of a wealthy businessman and civic leader to a beginning artist in the bohemian district of Munich and itinerate expatriate in Italy. While his particular circumstances were unique, he shared with millions of other Germans the experience of dramatic social upheaval and the threat of downward social mobility in the last decades of the nineteenth century. Within little more than a generation, Germany had attained political unification and had become an imperial power; industrialization and urbanization transformed the lives of those whose ancestors had tilled the soil for untold generations; hundreds of thousands turned their back on Europe in the hope of finding better luck in the New World. Men whose fathers and grandparents had lived comparatively stable lives faced unprecedented challenges in the workplace and at home. For all their eccentricity, the protagonists of Mann's early fiction capture a widespread sense of uncertainty among men who were no longer confident of their place in a changing world. Paolo Hoffmann, the artistically gifted but sickly protagonist of *The Will to Happiness* (*Der Wille zum Glück*, 1895), finally overcomes long-standing parental opposition and marries the woman he has pursued for years, only to die on the wedding night. While the protagonist of *Little Louise* dies on stage in the midst of a humiliating performance and Johannes Friedemann drowns, apparently lacking the will to lift his head from the water, the Joker comes to the morose conclusion that his life is so worthless that it does not deserve the drama of suicide.

Male insecurity found a welcome target in the women who threatened to break out of their traditional domestic roles as wives, mothers, and managers of the household economy. Beginning in the 1860s, women organized to demand access to better education, the right to work, and the right to vote. Friedrich Nietzsche set the tone for subsequent generations of male readers by denouncing the women's emancipation movement as a corruption of nature and a symptom of modern decadence. The Austrian Otto Weininger agreed, declaring in his widely influential treatise *Sex and Character* (*Geschlecht und Charakter*, 1903) that women are inferior beings who lack the capacity for reason and threaten to drag men down to their level. Seductive yet destructive women abound in German and Austrian art around 1900, including such figures as the evil sorceress Kundry in Wagner's *Parsifal* (1882), Frank Wedekind's Lulu, the amoral embodiment of female sexuality in the dramas *Earth-Spirit*

(*Erdgeist*, 1895) and *Pandora's Box* (*Die Büchse der Pandora*, 1904), and the prostitutes in Ludwig Kirchner's expressionist paintings.

The influential theorist Klaus Theweleit has argued that misogyny played a central role in modern German culture and contributed to the rise of a hyper-masculine, militarized society that culminated in German National Socialism.[5] Particularly suspect in the eyes of the German men were those who crossed the boundaries of traditional gender roles, including both assertive, "masculine" women and effeminate men. Thomas Mann's early fiction is replete with both types of characters, combining unmanly men with a series of *femmes fatales* who seem to enjoy nothing more than making men miserable. The hard-bitten actress who shatters the illusions of her young lover in *Fallen* is followed by several variations on the same theme: Gerda von Rinnlingen takes sadistic delight in the turmoil she arouses in Johannes Friedemann, who submits to her humiliations with masochistic pleasure – Gerda is brandishing a whip when she is first introduced. Equally evil is Amra, the female protagonist of *Little Louise*, who not only carries on a barely concealed affair with another man, but also plans with her lover the public humiliation of her husband.

The uncertainty surrounding gender roles in Mann's early fiction and his contemporary society carried over into anxiety about racial differences not only between Europeans and others abroad, but also between Jews and Christians at home. Germany began to acquire colonies only in the last decades of the nineteenth century, relatively late in comparison with other European nations, but expanded trade and travel had long since awakened interest in exotic places and peoples. Already in the late eighteenth century, Immanuel Kant and others speculated about the origins of racial difference and the number of racial types. Darwin's theory of evolution inspired new scientific and pseudo-scientific investigations. Physiognomists interpreted facial features, phrenologists probed skulls, and anthropologists measured brain sizes. Arthur de Gobineau wrote about the dangers of "miscegenation," while Houston Stewart Chamberlain proclaimed the superiority of the "Aryan" race. The discourse about race went hand in hand with debates about the "Jewish question" within Europe. Could or should Europe become a tolerant, multi-cultural society, accepting Jews as one of many distinct groups into its midst? Should Jews convert and conform to the norms of mainstream Christian culture? Or should they leave Europe in search of a Zionist homeland?

As the child of a partially Portuguese-Brazilian mother who later married an assimilated Jew, Mann was highly sensitive to questions of racial and religious difference, and both are reflected in his early fiction. Artistically sensitive male characters of questionable virility are frequently associated with the south, either through ancestry, travel, or both. The sickly Paolo Hoffmann of *The Will to Happiness* has a mother from South America, yellow skin, and dark hair that hangs in ringlets around his face; he spends years traveling in Italy and northern Africa. The Joker has a similar family background and also travels extensively in countries that border the Mediterranean. The child virtuoso in *Das Wunderkind* (1903) is a dark-skinned Greek who travels with an "Oriental" impresario. The dangerous female figures are also often marked by racial or religious difference: Paolo Hoffmann loves a nineteen-year-old beauty "of Semitic descent," but her mother is dismissed as "an ugly little Jew in a tasteless gray dress." Amra of *Little Louise* is described as a sensual odalisque with dark skin and voluptuous curves. Before her husband is forced to perform in drag, local students take the stage wearing blackface, bearing their teeth and howling barbarically.

The association of blackness and Jewishness with the forces of chaos will recur throughout Mann's fiction, as does a geographical symbolism that pits northern rationality and constraint against southern sickness and debauchery. His tendency to think in racial categories and to employ racial stereotypes in his fiction is one of the more troubling aspects of his work today, but also thoroughly typical of his times. One need only think of Gaugin's paintings of Tahitians as noble savages, or Picasso's portrait of Spanish prostitutes with the faces of African masks in *Les Demoiselles d'Avignon*. Mann's relation to the "Jewish question" is more complicated and fraught with our knowledge in hindsight of the genocide that took place in the course of Mann's lifetime. In many ways, Mann was a tolerant man, who declared himself on multiple occasions a friend of the Jews and who later condemned the Nazi persecution of the Jews in no uncertain terms. At the same time, however, Mann's diaries reveal the occasional anti-Semitic comment and he regularly introduces negative Jewish stereotypes into his literary works. As a result, Mann's relations with Jews and the Jewish characters in his fiction have been the subject of a fierce and ongoing debate.

Buddenbrooks: The Decline of a Family

On May 29, 1897 Samuel Fischer wrote to Thomas Mann in Italy to say that he would gladly publish a volume of his novellas. The book appeared the next year, with *Little Herr Friedemann* as the title story and five additional early works. In the same letter, Fischer mentioned that he would be able to provide a considerably larger honorarium for a novel, provided that it was of moderate length. Mann got to work immediately, suggesting that he may have been contemplating a longer project in any case. His first step was to conduct the necessary research: he studied the history of the Manns recorded by his grandfather and great-grandfather in the family bible and began pumping various family members for information. Mann's uncle, Wilhelm Marty, obliged with a series of detailed responses to Mann's questions about nineteenth-century Lübeck; his sister Julia wrote a long letter about their Aunt Elisabeth that Mann used almost verbatim for the figure of Tony Buddenbrook; even his mother provided traditional recipes that Mann used for descriptions of the lavish meals enjoyed by the Buddenbrook family. Mann began writing *Buddenbrooks* in Rome in October 1897; approximately one quarter of the novel was complete by the time he returned to Munich in April 1898. Work slowed as Mann moved several times within Munich, began working as an editor of the journal *Simplizissimus*, and continued to write the occasional novella, but he finally wrote the last sentence of the novel on July 18, 1900. A few weeks later he packaged up the sole handwritten copy of the novel, sealed it with wax (badly burning his hand in the process), and sent it off to Fischer in Berlin.

Months of waiting followed, during which Mann began his long-delayed year of compulsory military service. At the end of October, a letter from Samuel Fischer reached Mann in the garrison. Fischer indicated that he would publish the novel, but only if Mann were willing to cut its length in half. Mann responded with what he later described as the best letter that he ever wrote (now lost), in which he argued that the length was an essential component of the novel and that he was therefore unwilling to compromise. And after all, he reassured his publisher, this will not be the last novel that I write. More anxious months followed, until Fischer finally decided in early February 1901 to publish the novel in its entirety. It appeared in October of that year to largely favorable reviews; Mann was particularly pleased by Samuel Lublinski's review for the *Berliner Tageblatt*, in which he predicted that the novel "would grow with time and be read by many future generations." Initial sales were slow, but they accelerated when Fischer brought out an inexpensive edition in time for Christmas, 1902. *Buddenbrooks* has been a perennial bestseller ever since, both in the original German and in translation into all the world's major languages. The work that Mann completed shortly after his twenty-fifth birthday established him as one of Germany's leading writers and served as the basis of his lasting fame; decades later he was awarded the Nobel Prize for Literature largely on the strength of his first novel.

Buddenbrooks tells the story of the "decline of a family," as the subtitle suggests. It focuses on four generations of the Buddenbrook family in a city that is recognizable as Lübeck in everything but name. Like the Manns, on whose family history the novel is based, the fictional Buddenbrooks are a prominent family in the city and the owners of a thriving export business. The novel opens on a stormy October evening in 1835. Grandfather Johann Buddenbrook and his wife Antoinette, née Duchamps, have invited prominent local citizens to their new home on Meng Strasse (the actual house on the street of the same name in central Lübeck was owned by Mann's grandparents and currently houses a museum dedicated to the Mann family). Johann Buddenbrook is a jovial gentleman who exudes the combination of local patriotism and cosmopolitanism typical of Hanseatic Lübeck. He speaks a mixture of the local Low German dialect and French, powders his hair and wears old-fashioned knee-breeches, and has a taste for French gardens and Rococo art. While he is a religious skeptic in the tradition of the Enlightenment – the novel begins as he teases his granddaughter about the Lutheran catechism that she has memorized – his son, the Consul Johann (Jean) Buddenbrook, is a zealous Christian who takes the family business seriously and is an advocate of modern progress. His children are the major figures in the novel: Thomas (Tom) Buddenbrook, the ambitious older son who takes charge of the family business after his father's death, his dissolute brother Christian, and their sisters Antonie (Tony) and Clara. The fourth generation is represented in Tom's son Hanno, a sensitive, sickly youth who has an ear for music, but succumbs to typhus when he is only fifteen. When the novel ends in 1877, most of the Buddenbrook men are dead, the family business has been dissolved, and Christian has been institutionalized in a mental hospital.

With its vivid characterizations, crackling dialogue, and compelling plot, *Buddenbrooks* remains today as gripping a novel as when it was first released. Depending on the edition, *Buddenbrooks* stretches anywhere from 700 to 900 pages, but Mann broke the novel down into eleven books that are in turn subdivided into a series of shorter chapters, so that the otherwise daunting work can be consumed in easily digestible segments. Mann varies the tempo of the narration, which sometimes proceeds at a leisurely pace, as in the opening book that depicts a single dinner party in some fifty pages, and sometimes hurtles forward in scenes of riveting drama. Mann adapted the use of leitmotifs from Wagnerian opera to give thematic coherence and symbolic density to a novel that might otherwise have sprawled into a baggy monster. *Buddenbrooks* also plays on the full register of human emotions, ranging at various times from melancholy to sarcasm, farce to tragedy, philosophical contemplation to seething rage.

At the emotional core of *Buddenbrooks* lies the rivalry between the brothers Thomas and Christian. Mann based Thomas in part on his father and Christian on his father's younger brother Friedrich Wilhelm, Mann's "Uncle Friedel," who was not amused by his nephew's less-than-flattering portrait. "It is a sad bird that soils its own nest," he wrote on a postcard to his nephew Thomas, who confessed to momentary pangs of conscience in a letter to

Heinrich of January 8, 1904, but then consoled himself with the thought that he had devoted more time and energy to his uncle than anyone else ever had. What gives the relationship between Thomas and Christian Buddenbrook its emotional intensity, however, is the rivalry between Thomas and Heinrich Mann. As so often in Mann's work, there is a considerable amount of autobiographical identification between the author and his protagonist, although it is displaced into historical fiction.

On the surface, Thomas Buddenbrook plays the white sheep to his brother's black, the responsible businessman and respectable citizen versus the vagabond and ne'er-do-well Christian. Although Thomas lacks his parents' religious faith, he inherits the family's Protestant work-ethic. When his father dies unexpectedly, Thomas takes charge of the family business and, for a short time at least, brings it to unprecedented prosperity. He wins the respect of his peers and is elected to fill a vacancy in the senate that governs the city. Christian, in contrast, can neither hold a job nor command authority. As a boy, Christian displays a gift for mimicry and a love of the theater; he retains both talents as an adult, while developing a taste for women of ill repute. His interest in the family business, however, remains lukewarm at best. His father sends him to London in the hope of improving his business skills, and although Christian does manage to gain remarkable fluency in English, he spends most of his time at the theater. His business acumen is not improved by an eight-year stay in Valparaiso, Chile. Christian returns home with colorful stories of his adventures abroad and quickly resumes his dissipated life. When he dares to insult the integrity of the business world, Thomas erupts in uncontrolled anger, attacking his brother for his lack of self-discipline and accusing him of dragging the family's name into the mud. As gradually becomes clear, however, Thomas' fury derives in large part from the fact that Christian has succumbed to the forces that also gnaw at his own soul. As he becomes increasingly plagued by worries about his wife's possible infidelity, concerns about Hanno's lack of vitality, and a growing sense that his own life lacks meaning or purpose, Thomas struggles to maintain the façade of respectability until a seemingly minor toothache brings his life to a sudden and violent end.

Compounding the personal rivalry between the two brothers is an ongoing competition between the Buddenbrooks and the Hagenström family. The Hagenströms are relative newcomers in town, and although they are not widely liked, they display a ruthless vitality that contrasts with the growing enervation of the Buddenbrook clan. Early readers of *Buddenbrooks* – most notably the Marxist critic Georg Lukács[6] – saw in the fall of the Buddenbrooks and the rise of their rivals the triumph of the rapacious new capitalist bourgeoisie of the imperial age over the traditional burgher of the Hanseatic city-state. More

recent critics have argued convincingly that the Hagenströms and the Buddenbrooks are not fundamentally different at all: they strive for the same positions
of civic authority, conduct similar family businesses, and move in the same
social circles.[7] As in the case of the tension between Thomas and Christian, the
rivalry between the Buddenbrooks and the Hagenströms is fueled by a sense of
superficial difference masking a deep and undesired similarity.

Adding tension to the rivalry is the strong suggestion that the Hagenströms
are partially Jewish.[8] Herr Hagenström is said to have raised suspicions among
the local townspeople because of his marriage to a rich woman from Frankfurt
who wears large diamonds and has jet-black hair. His older son Hermann has
an unpleasant odor and a peculiarly shaped nose; his other son Moritz is sickly
but smart and becomes a shrewd lawyer. Tony Buddenbrook is particularly
outspoken about her hostility to the Hagenströms, referring to them as "das
Geschmeiß" (the dregs of society, scum), and either deliberately or uncon-
sciously referring to Laura Hagenström, née Semlinger, as *Sarah* Semlinger, a
typically Jewish name. Mann's notes used while writing *Buddenbrooks* reveal
that he based the Hagenströms on a Lübeck family named Fehling. "It was
this Fehling who married a Jew, née Oppenheimer," explained Julia Mann to
her brother Thomas in her long letter of September 1, 1897 about their Aunt
Elisabeth. In *Buddenbrooks*, Mann leaves the partially Jewish background of
the Hagenströms on the level of innuendo rather than open identification, but
the hints are broad enough that his contemporary readers would have easily
been able to read between the lines. In fact, one of Mann's bitterest foes, the
critic Adolf Bartels, complained in 1907 that Mann had allowed "an old German family to be defeated by a half-Jewish one – and it doesn't even bother
him!" Bartels was also quick to point out that Mann had married a Jew and
that his mother was "Portuguese, and thus perhaps not without Jewish or
Negro blood." More recent critics have viewed the Hagenströms as further evidence of Mann's anti-Semitism, although others have disputed this charge.[9]
Within the context of the novel, it seems safe to say that the Hagenströms have
a scapegoat function: they are the rivals onto which the Buddenbrooks can
project those aspects of themselves that they dislike.

The personal rivalries in *Buddenbrooks* play out against a political background in which the independent city-state and former capital of the Hanseatic
League is gradually transformed into a provincial town in the Prussian-
dominated German nation. In the opening scene, the men debate whether or
not their city should join the new Customs Union (*Zollverein*), an agreement of
the 1830s that removed trade barriers between the German provinces and thus
served as an economic precursor to political unification. Lübeck in fact did not
join the Union until 1868, reflecting a stubborn insistence on independence

that contributed to its growing isolation from the centers of German industrial and political power. In 1848, when angry mobs had taken to the barricades in Berlin in demand of democratic reforms, Consul Buddenbrook is able to placate the restless workers of Lübeck and reestablish the rule of law without violence, thus keeping the local civic order intact. Two decades later, however, Prussia led the way to unification with its military victories over Denmark, Austria, and France.

These political conflicts are mentioned only in passing in *Buddenbrooks*, but we see the direct influence of the new Prussian hegemony on Hanno Buddenbrook as he suffers through a long day at school toward the end of the novel. The institution that was once devoted to the classical education of the city's elite has been transformed into a quasi-military outpost reeking of male bravado. A series of authoritarian if inept teachers turn Hanno's school day into a living hell. Mann drew on his own unhappy experiences as a student in Lübeck when drawing the often wickedly funny caricatures of Hanno's teachers and depicting the antics of his unruly schoolmates, but Mann's work is also typical of other turn-of-the-century texts by those who endured the destructive discipline of the German and Austrian school systems. These include Robert Musil's *The Confusions of Young Törless* (*Die Verwirrungen des Zöglings Törleß*, 1906), Hermann Hesse's *Beneath the Wheel* (*Unterm Rad*, 1906), and Heinrich Mann's *Professor Unrat* (translated as *Small Town Tyrant*, literally "Professor Garbage," 1905), better known in the film version starring Marlene Dietrich, *The Blue Angel* (*Der Blaue Engel*, 1930).

Business and government are reserved for men in *Buddenbrooks*, but marital politics play an important role in the struggle for power between rival families. As members of the ruling class, the Buddenbrooks seek to improve their social status and enlarge their wealth through marriage, rather than allowing themselves to be swayed by passion or love – at least in theory. In practice, matters are more complicated. Monsieur Johann Buddenbrook, the family patriarch, had been deeply in love with his first wife, but she died after only a year giving birth to a son, Gotthold. His second marriage to the wealthy and respectable Antoinette Duchamps is based on mutual respect and good manners, but lacks passion. Gotthold outrages his otherwise tolerant father by marrying a woman of a low social status for love. Good sons must learn to discipline their desires: thus Thomas Buddenbrook breaks off his relationship with a shop girl and marries Gerda Arnoldsen, the daughter of a wealthy business partner. Christian, in contrast, is a "suitor," one of a number of dissolute men who associate with morally dubious women. He provokes his brother's undying wrath when he threatens to marry Aline Puvogel, a former prostitute who has his child, a breach of family ethics so egregious that Thomas finds it difficult to comprehend and impossible to forgive.

Tony Buddenbrook suffers most from the conflict between personal inclination and family duty surrounding marriage politics. In some ways she is the central figure in the novel, the only character present from the first page of *Buddenbrooks* to the last. We first meet Tony as a headstrong schoolgirl who enjoys the luxury of her maternal grandparents' villa on the edge of town, takes pride in the prestige of the Buddenbrook family, and conceives an undying hatred for Julchen Hagenström and her brothers. While on vacation at a seaside resort (clearly recognizable as Travemünde, although not named), Tony falls in love with Morten Schwarzkopf, a young university student and member of a radical fraternity (*Burschenschaft*), but Morten's humble origins as the son of a pilot boat captain render the prospect of marriage impossible. Her outraged father puts an end to the budding romance, with the full cooperation of Morten's father, and coerces Tony to marry the obsequious but seemingly solvent Hamburg businessman Bendix Grünlich. Tony divorces her husband when she discovers that he is actually bankrupt, but is again pressured by her family to marry the openly ridiculous Bavarian hops salesman Alois Permaneder. The second marriage also ends in divorce due to Permaneder's infidelity, his laziness, and Tony's inability or unwillingness to adapt to his alien Bavarian customs (Bavaria was literally a foreign country to a citizen of Lübeck before German unification). Tragedy strikes a third time when her daughter's husband, Hugo Weinschenk, is sent to prison for embezzlement and then abandons his family when released. In the end, Tony Buddenbrook is a victim of her own family pride and the willingness of her father and brother Thomas to manipulate that pride for what they perceive to be in the family's larger interest. Although it would be misguided to read *Buddenbrooks* as a feminist novel, it does reveal the price that women were forced or coerced to pay in the name of patriarchal family politics.

Death hangs heavy over the Buddenbrook family, gathering force with each successive generation until it crushes the life out of its final victim. The series of death scenes begins innocuously enough: Madame Antoinette Buddenbrook takes to her bed with what at first seems a mild illness, only to pass away with a peaceful sigh two weeks later. Her husband, Johann Buddenbrook, soon loses the will to live: he settles his affairs, passes leadership of the family firm on to his son, Consul Buddenbrook, and dies with the word "curious" on his lips. The calamities begin to accelerate midway through the novel: Consul Buddenbrook is found dead in his chair on a muggy summer afternoon; his older half-brother Gotthold dies of a heart attack in the arms of his wife; Clara, the young sister of Thomas, Tony, and Christian, succumbs to tuberculosis in distant Riga. Then death begins to hit home hard: the Consul's widow, Elisabeth, contracts pneumonia and dies a slow and horrifying death in the presence of the assembled family members. Thomas Buddenbrook leaves the dentist in agony after a failed tooth extraction, collapses on the street, and gurgles out his last breaths at home. Death attacks Thomas like a personal enemy, grabbing and smashing him into the cobblestones; his son, Hanno, in contrast, succumbs to an impersonal force. In a famous short chapter, Mann describes the typical if terrible pattern of typhoid fever as it leads its victim from headaches and high fever through agonizing pain, apathy, and false hope to inevitable death.

What causes the decline of the Buddenbrooks that Mann depicts with increasingly gruesome detail? It is tempting to view the tragic fate of their family as symptomatic of their social class, the downfall of the patrician burgher versus the corresponding rise of the capitalist bourgeoisie, but the evidence does not support this thesis. The Hagenströms thrive even as the Buddenbrooks deteriorate, although they are of the same social class, and we learn in the opening chapter that the Buddenbrooks are able to move into their stately new home because the previous owners, the Ratenkamps, had fallen into poverty and been forced to move away. The decline of the family would therefore seem to be a result of personal shortcomings, not the result of larger socio-historical developments. Here, too, however, the individual symptoms do not seem sufficient to cause the complete and utter devastation of the family: the Buddenbrooks suffer a series of financial setbacks, but they are not entirely bankrupt. They show evidence of moral turpitude – Christian's philandering, Thomas' willingness to enter into a shady business deal buying grain futures – but they are not the only citizens guilty of similar peccadilloes; Hugo Weinschenk has the misfortune to get caught for white-collar crimes that leave many others unscathed. Physical degeneration also plays a role, but Christian is more of a hypochondriac than someone with a chronic illness, and, as the astonished townspeople exclaim after Thomas Buddenbrook's collapse, no one dies of a toothache.

The various financial, ethical, and physical troubles of the Buddenbrook family are only symptoms of a general malaise, the feeling that it is too difficult to maintain the façade of purposeful striving when life is simply not worth living. Philosophical pessimism, not economic determinism, physiological degeneration, or moral depravity, is at the core of the Buddenbrooks' decline. Beneath the world of human endeavor, according to Schopenhauer, lies the unchanging, amoral force of the will. Faith in human reason and the belief in progress are illusions; we are in the grasp of forces that we can neither understand nor control. In terms of German literary history, *Buddenbrooks* is the modern antithesis to Gustav Freytag's *Debit and Credit* (*Soll und Haben*, 1855), a bestselling work of German realism about a young man who rises from rags to riches, becoming a partner in a successful family business and marrying the owner's daughter. From a European perspective, *Buddenbrooks* captures the sense of anti-bourgeois decadence made famous by Baudelaire's *Les Fleurs du mal* (1857), Huysmans' *À rebours* (1884), Klimt's paintings, and Ibsen's dramas.

Decadence and death are not the only forces at work in *Buddenbrooks*, however. Shortly before his fatal visit to the dentist, Thomas Buddenbrook has a revelatory reading experience of a passage on life after death in Schopenhauer's *The World as Will and Representation*. Schopenhauer's name is not mentioned, and, according to the editors of the new critical edition of Thomas Mann's work, there is some doubt as to whether Mann had studied Schopenhauer directly at this point of his career, as he subsequently claimed, or whether he knew his works indirectly, through Nietzsche and Wagner. What matters in this context is that Thomas Buddenbrook derives a very Nietzschean conclusion from his foray into Schopenhauer's philosophy. That is, he responds to the contention that individual human existence is a "mistake," an entrapment into individuality from which only death brings release, not with a morbid desire to succumb to death, but rather with an affirmation of life. According to his somewhat feverish logic, Thomas is convinced that he will become one with the life-force of others after his death, but also that the ones who will be the most vital participants in the communal afterlife are those who lived this life most intensely as individuals. Implicitly following the argument that Nietzsche formulates in his *Genealogy of Morals*, Thomas Buddenbrook turns Schopenhauer's yearning to relinquish the will into an affirmation of desire – an affirmation, to be sure, expressed in the language of nihilism: "Better to desire nothingness, than not to desire at all." Even this bleak insight quickly fades, however, as Thomas Buddenbrook and his family spiral downward to their seemingly inevitable demise.

[handwritten marginal note, left margin, rotated: "people don't want to die but death affirms life death means there was a life"]

TM born on 1875

Artists and outcasts in Mann's early fiction

From the outside looking in, things were going very well indeed for Thomas Mann in the years between the publication of *Buddenbrooks* in October 1901 and the outbreak of the First World War. While the reputation of Mann's first novel continued to grow, just as Samuel Lublinski had predicted, new publications followed: *Tonio Kröger* won widespread acclaim when it appeared in February 1903. Later that year it was included in a second volume of novellas with *Tristan* as the title story. Mann's drama *Fiorenza* was published in 1905, a second novel, *Royal Highness*, in 1909, and in 1912, *Death in Venice* was hailed as an instant classic. Mann's personal life seemed to be keeping pace with his brilliant career. In February 1905 he married Katia Pringsheim, the daughter of one of the richest and most socially prominent families in Munich. Nine months later his daughter Erika was born, to be followed in rapid succession by Klaus (1906), Angelus (Golo, 1909), and Monika (1910); Elisabeth (1918) and Michael (1919) would come later. With the financial assistance of his in-laws, Mann was able to move into a seven-room apartment complete with a baby grand piano; a few years later he had a vacation home built south of Munich in Bad Tölz, where he spent summers with his growing family; in 1912 the Mann family moved into a palatial villa on the outskirts of Munich.

From the inside looking out, however, life was difficult for Thomas Mann. In the years prior to his marriage, Mann was deeply and hopelessly in love with Paul Ehrenberg, a young painter who decades later would serve as the model for Rudi Schwerdtfeger in *Doctor Faustus*. Married life also had its difficulties: in addition to adjusting to his new roles as husband and father, Mann had to endure frequent visits from his in-laws (relations with Katia's father, Alfred Pringsheim, were particularly tense), who not only lived in the neighborhood, but also installed a telephone in the apartment that intruded into Mann's precious solitude. Relations with Heinrich were growing worse. Heinrich did not attend his brother's wedding and his visit to Bad Tölz with his first wife, Inés Schmied, in the summer of 1908 was a disaster. "I still see your brother's face," wrote Inés to Heinrich shortly thereafter, "as he stared into the air so coldly, indifferently, and yet uncomfortably ... I'd rather be dead than live there."[1] Two years later Thomas' sister Carla committed suicide.

Despite growing fame and the unqualified triumph of *Tonio Kröger* and *Death in Venice*, Mann's literary career was not going as well as he would have liked. For an author who in later years prided himself on his ability to complete long novels, the decade before the war had more than its share of frustration. Plans for a novel named *Maja* were never realized; a major essay on "Intellect and Art" ("Geist und Kunst") remained a fragment, as did an essay on Frederick the Great – Mann would attribute these works to Gustav von Aschenbach in *Death in Venice*. Other works were not completed until many years later: at the outbreak of the First World War, only a few chapters of both *The Magic Mountain* and *Felix Krull* had been written, while *Doctor Faustus* existed only as the germ of an idea jotted into a notebook. Even completed works did not always live up to the highest standards of Mann's art: despite interesting ideas, *Fiorenza* is a failure as a drama, as the characters tend to speak in page-long paragraphs of convoluted prose, and while *Royal Highness* garnered generally polite reviews, it clearly did not rise to the level of *Buddenbrooks*.

Tonio Kröger

In the autobiographical essay "On Myself" (1940), Mann referred to *Tonio Kröger* as his favorite work; he stated elsewhere that it was the one that was closest to his heart (*mein Eigentlichstes*). The substantial novella focuses on the relationship between the artist and society that was central to Mann's early fiction and, in many ways, to his entire career. *Tonio Kröger's* origins can be traced back to September 1899, when Mann traveled from Munich to Denmark for a two-week vacation. Vague ideas were already beginning to take shape later that fall, but it was not until 1902 that he began to write. "I wrote it very slowly," Mann recalled in "On Myself," noting that the central theoretical section took him months to complete. It was received warmly by Mann's contemporaries, and it has remained one of Mann's best-known and best-loved stories.

The novella falls into three parts, although it is divided into nine short chapters. We are introduced to Tonio Kröger as a fourteen-year-old schoolboy in love with the popular Hans Hansen; two years later, he is infatuated with Ingeborg Holm. The second part consists of a long theoretical discussion between Kröger, now about thirty, and his artist-friend, the Russian Lisaweta Iwanowna, in Munich. The novella concludes when Kröger journeys north to vacation in Denmark, stopping in his hometown along the way. As in the case of *Buddenbrooks*, the town is not explicitly identified, but it is easily recognizable as Lübeck; other autobiographical elements include the combination of a stern north German father with a sensuous mother from the south, the bohemian milieu of Munich, and the trip to Denmark. Mann in fact encouraged autobiographical interpretations of the work and occasionally signed letters, no doubt half in jest, as "Tonio K." As always, however, Mann makes his confessions behind the mask of fiction: his mother did not remarry after his father's death, there was no real-life equivalent of Lisaweta Iwanowna, and Mann almost certainly did not indulge in years of sexual debauchery while living in Italy. As Tonio Kröger puts it, the artist who is not working is "like an actor with his makeup off; who has no identity when he is not performing."[2] The phrase captures nicely the combination of autobiography and theatricality in Mann's fiction, role playing that creates the impression of confessional intimacy.

The notion that the artist is an outsider in bourgeois society has its roots in German romanticism. Goethe's Werther, Eichendorff's *Taugenichts* (literally "good-for-nothing"), and the lyric "I" of Heine's *Book of Songs* (*Buch der Lieder*) are all portrayed – or portray themselves – as sensitive, artistically inclined individuals who are distinguished from the boring "Philistines" around them by their capacity for both ecstasy and irony. Kindred spirits to these figures – all in works with which Mann was familiar – were Shakespeare's Hamlet, the indecisive outsider who also plays an important role in Goethe's *Wilhelm Meister*, the figure of Cain from the Old Testament (the narrator refers to the stigmatizing mark on Tonio Kröger's brow), and Nietzsche's Zarathustra.

While thus working within a long literary tradition, Mann defines the difference of the artist in his own peculiar way. Like his author, Tonio Kröger experiences downward social mobility. Tonio grows up in the most impressive house in the city where his father is a leading citizen, but the father dies, the house is sold, and the family business liquidated. When Kröger returns to his hometown as a respected writer but without a passport, he is confused with a criminal and almost arrested. Tonio Kröger is further stigmatized by what is described as his racial mixture: his father is a tall, blue-eyed north German with an erect posture and a stern sense of self-discipline, whereas his mother, Consuelo, is a passionate dark-haired beauty. Tonio Kröger will struggle to reconcile the conflicting impulses toward duty and inclination that are not only symbolized by his curious name, but literally programmed into his blood. The blurring of lines between cultural difference and biological *burgher* → a citizen of a town or a city, typically a member of the wealthy bourgeoisie.

36   *The Cambridge Introduction to Thomas Mann*

determinism was typical of the time and played an important role in Mann's self-understanding. Sexual deviance combines with class distinction and racial difference to define Tonio Kröger as a social outcast. Mann based the story of Tonio's unrequited love for Hans Hansen on his own adolescent passion for a boy named Armin Martens. While there is nothing overtly sexual about Tonio's friendship with Hans, there is a fervent yearning for acceptance combined with the melancholy awareness of its impossibility that infuses the scene with a barely concealed homoerotic tension. Two years later Tonio encounters a caricatured self-portrait in the flamboyantly gay dance instructor François Knaak, who ridicules his student as "Fräulein Kröger" when Tonio mistakenly ends up with the girls in the midst of his lesson. "Can one even say that an artist *is* a man?" wonders Tonio in his discussion with Lisaweta; "I think we artists are all in rather the same situation as those artificial papal sopranos … Our voices are quite touchingly beautiful. But –" (p. 156).

Many of Tonio Kröger's romantic predecessors are distinguished by their artistic sensibility and yet are incapable of producing art. Goethe's Werther is typical in this regard: "I couldn't draw now, not a line," he writes in his letter of May 10, 1771, "and I have never been a better painter than in these moments." Tonio Kröger will struggle to resolve this paradox. While Werther revels in the glorious spring day, Tonio Kröger claims that spring makes him nervous because it awakens emotions that make artistic production impossible. Art must be coldly analytical, in his opinion; otherwise it becomes sentimental, heartfelt, and banal. Being an artist is a curse in that it alienates one from the unselfconscious enjoyment of life, and yet it is also a holy calling, an ascetic discipline that elevates one above one's own passions and those of people who go about their daily business unburdened by the demands of art. And yet Tonio Kröger remains unconvinced by his own rhetoric, as he is taken aback by Lisaweta's simple statement that he is just a burgher after all, "a burgher gone astray, a lost and confused burgher" (*ein verirrter Bürger*).

Tonio Kröger's return to the north helps him to find his way. At the resort in Denmark he is observing preparations for a dinner dance when he sees Hans Hansen and Ingeborg Holm walk through the room. As the narrator suggests, they are not literally the same individuals whom Tonio once knew, but manifestations of a certain blue-eyed and blond-haired "racial type." The party unfolds as an uncanny repetition of events familiar from Tonio's troubled youth, complete with a dance and an awkward girl who stumbles and falls. Tonio Kröger watches with bitter-sweet emotions and eventually retires to sob in his bed in a flood of self-pity. In the next scene, however, we discover that Tonio Kröger has had an epiphany. In a letter to Lisaweta, he explains once again that he can never be part of the bourgeois world, but now he not only accepts the fact that he loves that world, but he also realizes that in that love lies the strength of his art. In literary–historical terms, Tonio Kröger – and through him, his author Thomas Mann – distances himself from the cold aestheticism of Flaubert, the heartless cruelty and unbridled sensuality of Heinrich Mann's Renaissance cult, and the sentimental celebrations of hearth and home that were popular at the time as *Heimatliteratur*. The result is a programmatic novella that not only hovers between modernism and tradition, but also incorporates theoretical reflections on its innovative poetic practice into the text.

Artists, ascetics, and outcasts

Fiorenza, Mann's only completed drama, and the closely related novella *Gladius Dei* transform the sympathetic portrait of the artist as a young man into studies of fanatical obsession. Mann's historical drama is set in Florence, Italy in 1492. It centers on the conflict between the dying Lorenzo de Medici, famous patron of Renaissance art, and the ascetic Prior Hieronymus, known to history as Girolamo Savonarola, the Dominican priest who called for a bonfire of the vanities and ended up being burned at the stake instead. Mann shifts the setting to his contemporary Munich in the novella *Gladius Dei*, in which another monk named Hieronymus – described as a dead ringer for his famous Florentine predecessor – takes issue with an all-too-sensuous depiction of the Virgin Mary displayed in the window of a Munich boutique. The monk demands with increasing vehemence that the offending image be removed from public view until he is forcibly evicted from the store. "*Gladius Dei super terram*," he mutters, shaking his fist, "*cito et velociter!*" (Soon and fast the sword of God will come down to earth [to punish the city's sinners]).[3]

Thomas Mann was in Florence during the four hundredth anniversary of Savonarola's execution in 1898 and he kept a picture of Savonarola on his desk through his life. His interest in Savonarola reflected both his attitude toward art and his ambivalent feelings about Italy. Mann traveled to Italy five times between 1895 and 1902, where he stayed for extended periods, including one long stretch from October 1896 to April 1898. Unlike Heinrich, however, Thomas Mann never felt entirely at home in the south. "All that *bellezza* (beauty) gets on my nerves" (p. 164), says Tonio Kröger to Lisaweta as he gets ready to vacation in Denmark, echoing at least in part the sentiments of his author. Mann harbored similar reservations about Munich. Although he lived for decades in the Bavarian capital, he always retained a certain critical detachment from it – just as his Joseph never forgets that he is a Hebrew after decades in Egypt. Mann had already created a memorable parody of southern Germany in *Buddenbrooks*, where Tony flees her second husband, Alois Permaneder, and the lazy, beer-soaked Bavaria that he represents.

The opening pages of *Gladius Dei* would seem to present an idyllic image of Munich as an artistic and intellectual Mecca. The sun is shining on a beautiful day in June. Music pours out from open windows onto streets where young people casually whistle motifs from Wagner's operas as they stroll with the latest literary journals tucked under their arms. Whimsical statues adorn buildings full of ateliers and boutiques selling everything from antiquities to modern art. "Munich was resplendent" (*München leuchtete*) (p. 75). The first line of Mann's novella captures the pride of a city that liked to view itself as the "Athens on the Isar" or the "Florence of the North," and the phrase was later adopted as a semi-official slogan of the city. Had the civic leaders read Mann's story more closely, they might have hesitated in their choice, for the depiction of art-loving Munich soon slips toward implicit criticism. Two "young men of classical education, well versed in the arts and other learning" (p. 81) stand outside an art boutique and make lewd comments about the sexy Madonna in the window; inside, a gentleman in a yellow suit with a devilish goatee cackles over presumably erotic French drawings, while an Englishman admires a small statue of a coquettish prepubescent girl that verges on child pornography. He is attended by the unctuous shop owner, Blüthenzweig, whose name and nose that "lay rather flat on his upper lip" (p. 83) strongly suggest that he is a Jew; Mann uses precisely the same phrase to describe Hermann Hagenström's nose in *Buddenbrooks*. Art-loving Munich turns out to be populated by calculating Jewish shopkeepers – Blüthenzweig seems to sniff his customers as he serves them – who cater to the taste of their lecherous male customers.

The monk Hieronymus brandishes his metaphorical sword of God against these decadent aesthetes with a moral fury that also moves in the direction of parody. Tonio Kröger had come to terms with his conflicting impulses in the understanding that his art drew its strength from his love for a life that he could not share, an insight that leaves him with "longing, and sad envy, just a touch of contempt, and a whole world of innocent delight" (p. 192). In *Gladius Dei* and *Fiorenza*, in contrast, there is nothing innocent about artistic bliss. Savonarola is consumed by a divine fire that drives him to condemn the city and eventually leads to his own immolation in *Fiorenza*; *Gladius Dei* offers a semi-comic, slightly grotesque variant on the same theme, as Hieronymus has to be dragged out of the store, his face twitching with desperate hatred and uncontrollable rage as he fulminates against sensuality and art.

The various incarnations of Savonarola provide Mann with another distorted mask for his confessional art. To a certain extent, Mann identifies with Savonarola: "Art is the sacred torch," exclaims Hieronymus, "that must shed its

Handwritten margin notes: Scourge: punish / flagellates: flog (someone), either as a religious discipline or sexual gratification.

merciful light into all life's terrible depths, into every shameful and sorrowful abyss" (p. 87). Mann stylizes his struggle to control his unruly sexual impulses into a fictional conflict of biblical proportions, in which the artist becomes a holy prophet who scourges the people even as he flagellates himself into a creative fury. But there is always an element of irony in Mann, a self-critical awareness that artistic inspiration and ascetic self-discipline can easily slide into grandiloquence and megalomania. Savonarola is a self-portrait and a self-caricature, but also a critique of Mann's self-important contemporaries such as Stefan George, who was basking in the admiration of his sycophantic acolytes while Mann honed his chiseled prose. In the spring of 1904, Ludwig Derleth, one of George's followers, invited Mann to a reading of his pseudo-prophetic "Proclamations." Mann accepted the invitation and turned the experience into the short story *With the Prophet* (*Beim Propheten*, 1904). In this work, Mann sends his alter ego, a writer whose book is currently being read in middle-class circles (*Buddenbrooks*), to attend a reading among decadent bohemians on the dodgy outskirts of town. In a room decorated with portraits of Luther, Nietzsche, Robespierre, and Savonarola, a disciple of the prophetic poet Daniel reads fervently from his master's proclamations, concluding the evening by sending forth his "soldiers … to plunder – the world!" A few years earlier Mann had depicted another mad prophet in the figure of Lobgott Piepsam, and the fanatical poet Daniel zur Höhe will return in Doctor Faustus as a harbinger of the madness soon to be unleashed by Hitler and his followers.

In *Tristan*, the artist appears not as a grandiloquent prophet, but as a dilettantish poseur. The story takes place in a sanatorium, a location that Mann would later make famous in *The Magic Mountain*. The north German businessman Anton Klöterjahn brings his ailing wife, Gabriele, to the clinic, remains for a few days, but then returns home with his baby son. During her stay at the sanatorium Gabriele becomes interested in a writer named Detlev Spinell. One day when most of the patients are away on an outing, Gabriele and Spinell stay behind. At his urging she plays a theme from Wagner's *Tristan and Isolde* on the piano; he falls to his knees before her, but she leaves the room and soon begins to cough up blood. Her husband is summoned. Detlev Spinell insults him, but before the two men come to blows, Gabriele dies.

On one level, *Tristan* is a burlesque of Wagner's opera, with Klöterjahn in the role of King Mark, Gabriele as Isolde, and Spinell as Tristan, although in this case the infidelity never goes beyond the shared passion for Wagner's music. Elements of *Buddenbrooks* are present as well: Gabriele is from the Hanseatic city of Bremen. Her father is a businessman, but he also plays the violin, prompting Spinell to observe that sometimes a declining family of respectable burghers is transfigured by art in its final days. Klöterjahn and his baby boy, in contrast, display the boisterous vitality of Hermann Hagenström and his sons. From Spinell's perspective, Klöterjahn is almost disgustingly healthy: he packs in hearty meals at the sanatorium, looks after his equally robust son, and flirts with the nurses – *Klöten* is north German slang for testicles. Detlev Spinell is Klöterjahn's opposite in every way: he has rotten teeth, no facial hair, and cannot look women in the eye. While Klöterjahn works, Spinell "writes" – although it turns out that aside from one thin novel with suspiciously large print, he writes only letters, not fiction, and, as far as Gabriele can tell, he writes far more letters than he receives. Once again, Mann projects certain aspects of himself onto the figure of Detlev Spinell. Even in the best of times, Mann wrote slowly, particularly in comparison with Heinrich, who was publishing at a furious pace while Mann struggled to find his artistic bearings after completing *Buddenbrooks*. At times, Mann took pride in the slow but steady rate of his literary production; at others, it became a source of torment. His attitude toward Heinrich's facile productivity alternated correspondingly between envy and scorn: "It is immoral to write one bad book after the next," Mann wrote in his notebook in early 1905.

In *Difficult Hour* and *Death in Venice*, Mann portrays artists who produce heroically despite great difficulties; in *Tristan*, however, Mann depicts a self-absorbed "artist" who produces no art. Unlike the transparently autobiographical protagonists of *The Joker* and *Tonio Kröger*, however, the artistic poseur in *Tristan* is described in ways that make him seem strange, despite certain similarities with his author. More precisely, he is coded in ways that suggest he is Jewish. Mann's narrator begins by forgetting Spinell's name, which he recalls only as "some sort of a mineral or precious stone";[4] he has a thick, fleshy nose; he has a strange way of speaking; and he comes from Lemberg. Decoded, the clues read as follows: the reference to the name as a mineral or gem may prompt the reader to think of such "typically Jewish" names as Stein or Bernstein; according to Mann's German editors, a *Spinell* is also a semi-precious stone. The forgetting or repressing of the specific name also suggests that we are being encouraged to think in terms of a certain type rather than an individual. Lemberg is known today as L'vov, a city in western Ukraine that was the capital of Galicia in the Austro-Hungarian Empire and home to a large number of Jews, many of whom fled west to escape pogroms. In Western Europe, these *Ostjuden* (eastern European Jews) stood out because they dressed differently and had foreign speech patterns, a way of speaking known disparagingly as *mauscheln*. The prominent nose speaks for itself.

In light of these multiple hints, why the coyness on the part of Mann's narrator? Why not simply say: Detlev Spinell was a *mauschelnder Ostjude* pretending to be an artist? There are two interrelated reasons: first, to identify

Spinell overtly as a Jew would be superfluous, given the many hints; second, by not openly identifying Spinell as a Jew, Mann leaves open the possibility that the alien "artist" is an indirect self-portrait after all. Mann also had a prominent nose that was often exaggerated in caricatures, and, like Spinell, Mann was something of a dandy in his dress and a writer who often found it difficult to write. Identifying Spinell openly as an eastern European Jew would have been to make him obviously foreign; by leaving the hints at the level of hints, and combining the portrait of the Jew with aspects of himself, Mann creates a distorted self-image as a (Jewish) dilettante. The Jew does double duty as the alien other and as a projection of negative aspects of the self. Spinell is also sexually ambiguous, a man with no beard who is attracted to and yet afraid of women.

Marriage and the artist

Two years after *Tristan* was published, Mann was a married man with his first child on the way. For a student of Nietzsche, who had jested in *The Genealogy of Morals* that a married philosopher belonged in a comedy, and particularly for a man with an abiding desire for handsome young men, getting used to the role of the married artist was not easy. On the other hand, Mann had good reasons to marry, and particularly good reasons to marry Katia Pringsheim. Marriage allowed Mann to put an end to the love for Paul Ehrenberg that he knew could go nowhere and that had become a source of ongoing torment. Marriage was also a way to prove to the public, and perhaps also to convince himself, that his sexual orientation was "normal" after all. The desire to emulate his father's respectability, at least outwardly, also played a role in Mann's decision to marry. Katia Pringsheim was one of the most eligible young women in Munich. Only twenty years old when Mann began to pursue her (he was twenty-eight at the beginning of their courtship, twenty-nine when they married), Katia was attractive, vivacious, and exceptionally intelligent. She was one of the first women in Munich to pass the *Abitur* and was studying mathematics at the university when they met. She was also gifted at languages and spoke better English and French than he ever did. Katia's father was a professor of mathematics and independently wealthy. The family owned a spectacular mansion in the heart of Munich that was the social hub of a network of artists and intellectuals. That the Pringsheims were assimilated Jews was not unusual in this milieu. Mann's publisher, Samuel Fischer, was Jewish, as were many of his critics and a substantial portion of his reading public. And besides, the Pringsheims did not seem particularly Jewish: "One never thinks of Jewishness among these people," wrote Mann to Heinrich on February 27, 1904; "you only sense culture." Katia and her twin brother Klaus had been baptized at an early age and only gradually became aware of their family's Jewish origins; in later years Katia Mann vigorously denied that she was Jewish.

The case of the Pringsheim family raises larger questions concerning Jewish assimilation in Germany and Mann's relations with the Jews. When was a Jew no longer a Jew? Heinrich Heine had converted in the 1820s, viewing conversion as the entry ticket to German society, but found to his bitter disappointment that he remained a Jew in the eyes of German Christians. Katia's parents, Alfred and Hedwig Pringsheim, lived their lives as baptized Christians in Munich, but they were still forced to flee Hitler's Germany as Jews in their old age. Mann's comment to Heinrich indicates that he was aware of the Pringsheim family background, but eager to downplay its significance. In this passage, he emphasizes their high cultural status; elsewhere Mann stressed the slightly exotic appeal of his wife, stylizing her into an "Oriental princess" in the autobiographical poem *Song of the Little Child* (*Gesang vom Kindchen*, 1919), the fitting bride for an artist of mixed race, as he liked to view himself. The fact that Mann had worked briefly for an anti-Semitic journal in the mid 1890s and that his fiction includes some negative Jewish stereotypes nevertheless suggests that there were tensions beneath the surface of his blithe comment to Heinrich about the Pringsheims' lack of obviously "Jewish" characteristics; his mother was also unhappy that Katia wanted only a civil ceremony, as she felt that now was the time for the Pringsheims to prove that they were really Protestants.

Mann would work through some of the issues raised by his marriage in his portrait of Schiller as a recently married artist in *Difficult Hour*, in his sensational novella *Wälsungenblut* about incestuous Jewish twins, and in the romantic comedy of his second novel, *Royal Highness*. Before moving to the discussion of these texts, however, a final comment on Mann's marriage in the light of his sexual orientation seems warranted. Given the revelations of the diaries, it is easy to categorize Mann as a homosexual, and to assume therefore that he married for strategic reasons only – for money, status, and to secure a smokescreen behind which to hide his illicit desires. Human sexuality is nothing if not complicated, however, and does not always fit neatly into clearly defined categories. Mann had flirted briefly with the possibility of marrying an English woman whom he had met a few years earlier in Italy; he occasionally notes attractive women as well as men in his diaries, and he did father six children. It is therefore not implausible that beneath all the calculations that made Katia Pringsheim seem an appropriate marriage partner there was also an element of physical attraction, even heterosexual desire. In any case, as Mann argued in his 1925 essay on "Marriage in Transition" ("Die Ehe im Übergang"), marriage is based on more than sexual attraction; it is also companionship strengthened over time by common experiences and children. There is no need to become overly sentimental about Mann's marriage, which had its share of difficulty and tension, but it was a partnership that worked for more than fifty years and, as Mann stressed in his speech to Katia on the occasion of her seventieth birthday, an essential part of his life.

Mann wrote *Schwere Stunde* in March and April 1905, shortly after his wedding on February 11 and honeymoon in Zurich. It was a commissioned work, written for a special issue of the journal *Simplicissimus* to commemorate the one hundredth anniversary of Schiller's death. Mann portrays the thirty-seven-year-old Schiller as he struggles to write the historical drama *Wallenstein*. Schiller is wracked by a chronic cough, filled with doubts about how to proceed with his work, and consumed by envy of Goethe – named only as "the other one in Weimar" – who creates his works of genius with seemingly effortless ease. In the end, however, Schiller sits down to write, driven by ambition and inspired by his love for his wife: "Maybe it wouldn't be good, but it would be finished. And when it was finished, behold! – it was good, too." The short novella can be read – once again – as a coded depiction of Mann's struggle with Heinrich, as Mann turns the slow pace of his own literary production into a virtue and condemns "scribblers and dilettantes who do not live under the pressure and discipline of talent." Perhaps more important, however, is Mann's identification with Schiller in this novella. Goethe and Schiller had enormous cultural status in Germany at the time. They were venerated not only as great writers, but as national heroes. Mann's novella is in praise of these cultural icons but also an implicit effort to establish himself as their legitimate heir. Mann's desire to be Germany's representative author motivated several other projects during these years: the fragmentary "Intellect and Art" was intended as the sequel to Schiller's famous essay "On Naïve and Sentimental Poetry"; Mann also planned to write a novel about Frederick the Great, another national hero, and he devoted his energies to *Fiorenza* at least in part because drama was of higher cultural status than the novel in Wilhelminian Germany, and because Mann's chief rival for the position of Germany's unofficial poet laureate, Gerhard Hauptmann, had distinguished himself as a dramatist.

If Mann's first project after his marriage was calculated to elevate his cultural status, his second seemed destined to get him in trouble. Like *Tristan*, the novella *Wälsungenblut* is directly linked to a Wagnerian opera. *Die Walküre* (*The Valkyrie*) is the second opera of the Ring cycle. Under the assumed name of Wälse, the Norse God Wotan had an affair with a mortal woman. She gave birth to the twins Siegmund and Sieglinde, who were separated soon after birth. *Die Walküre* begins as Siegmund seeks shelter from his enemies in what turns out to be the home of his sister, now married to the brutal Hunding. Sieglinde cares for the exhausted refugee in a scene filled with growing sexual tension. Her husband returns home and grudgingly allows the stranger to spend the night. Sieglinde drugs Hunding into a deep sleep and returns to Siegmund, who gradually reveals his identity. They are both the children of "Wälse"! "You are my sister and my bride," exclaims an enraptured Siegmund, and the act comes to a shocking conclusion as brother and sister fall into an incestuous embrace.

In his retelling of the story, Mann shifts the setting to a family in his contemporary Munich that looks suspiciously like the Pringsheims. Sieglinde Aarenhold, who is engaged to Herr von Beckerath, attends a performance of Wagner's *Walküre* with her twin brother Siegmund; after the performance they imitate their namesakes by committing incest. "And what about Beckerath?" asks Sieglinde afterwards. "We've robbed him" (*Beganeft haben wir ihn*), responds Siegmund contemptuously, "the Goy!" With the use of the Yiddish words "Goy" and "beganeft,"[5] Mann confirms what would have been obvious to his contemporary readers all along: he has transformed Wagner's Germanic heroes into Jews. The father is from Eastern Europe and is said to have made his fortune by unspecified but suspicious "schemings" (p. 293); his ridiculously overdressed wife still speaks in the guttural accent of her youth. While the older generation is thus identified as only partially assimilated *Ostjuden*, their children seem hyper-German: the older brother wears a decorated military uniform and has dueling scars on his cheeks; the twins speak a precise, affected German and are opera buffs with Wagnerian names. Deep down, however, Sieglinde and Siegmund Aarenhold remain as different as the demigods in Wagner's opera, for they, too, are "strange, of a breed and kind hopelessly different from them" (*von fremder, von hoffnungslos anderer Art als die anderen*) (p. 306).

Was Thomas Mann making fun of his new Jewish in-laws? Was he seeking revenge in literature for the awkwardness that he may have felt as the Christian suitor (Beckerath) to Katia, twin sister of Klaus Pringsheim? Rumors to this effect began to circulate in Munich. Mann had already reluctantly complied with his editor's request that he replace Siegmund's final jab at Beckerath with a more innocuous and less obviously Jewish line; now he gave in to his father-in-law's insistence that he withdraw the story from publication before it could cause a scandal for the Pringsheim family. *Wälsungenblut* nevertheless leaked out when a bookstore employee discovered that the printed pages of the withdrawn story had been used as scrap paper. In later years, the story continued to exist on the margins of Mann's *oeuvre*: in the early 1920s, he authorized a limited luxury edition of the work and an English translation was published in the 1930s. The novella was included in the posthumous edition of Mann's works, but without the original ending; only the new critical edition has restored the Yiddish insult of the original text. The initial controversy swirling around the novella has continued unabated: does the text expose Mann as a dyed-in-the-wool racist anti-Semite? Is it only a momentary lapse on the part of an individual who for the most part had a good record of befriending and defending Jews against anti-Semitic persecution? Or is *Wälsungenblut* a sly – perhaps all-too-sly – attempt to ridicule the notoriously anti-Semitic Richard Wagner by suggesting that there is no essential difference between Wotan's mythical children and a pair of effete incestuous Jews in downtown Munich?

We stand on less controversial ground when we turn to the third work inspired by Mann's marriage, the novel *Royal Highness*. It begins with the birth of Prince Klaus Heinrich, who is second in line to the throne of a small, unnamed principality somewhere in Mann's contemporary Germany. The young prince is shy, both because his royal birth makes it impossible for him to mingle freely with his subjects and because he has a deformed left arm that he does his best to conceal. He nevertheless discovers as a young man that he has a talent for performing his representative role in public and gradually takes over his older brother's ceremonial duties. The people are fond of their prince, but the local economy is in shambles and he can do nothing to help. A serendipitous solution is found when the American millionaire Samuel Spoelmann decides to retire in their kingdom, revitalizing the economy with an infusion of new money. Klaus Heinrich falls in love with Spoelmann's daughter, Imma; they marry and will presumably live happily ever after. Or rather, they will share a *moderately* pleasant life: "an austere happiness" (*ein strenges Glück*).[6]

It is easy enough to read *Royal Highness* as another of Mann's attempts to come to terms in his fiction with his recent marriage, but this time in a comic mode. The happy ending recalls the triumphant chorus in celebration of marriage that concludes the *Meistersinger*, and Mann later admitted that he was thinking of Wagner's opera as he was writing *Royal Highness*. All the major characters in the novel have their real-life correspondents, although Katia Mann claimed that the portrait of her father as Samuel Spoelmann was more accurate than that of herself as Imma.[7] The protagonist is another indirect self-portrait, but Klaus was also the name of Mann's brother-in-law, Heinrich that of his brother, and Klaus Heinrich Thomas Mann the full name of Mann's oldest son, born November 18, 1906 as Mann was writing *Royal Highness*.

While the incestuous twins in *Wälsungenblut* can be seen as caricatures of Katia and Klaus Pringsheim distorted into negative Jewish stereotypes, Imma Spoelmann is charmingly exotic in a way that is reminiscent of Mann's mother: her paternal grandfather married a woman from South America who is said to have been a Portuguese Creole with a drop of indigenous blood. Her father married a half-English woman, who gave birth to Imma, "that wonderful blood-mixture of a girl" (p. 174). Prince Klaus Heinrich's role as the principality's figurehead corresponds with Mann's self-understanding as Germany's representative writer, although certainly with a touch of irony, as Klaus Heinrich understands little of the people he represents and can do nothing to solve their problems. The withered left hand can be read as an indirect reference to Mann's general sense of stigmatization or, more specifically, a coded reference to his repressed homosexuality, although it also contains a historical allusion to Kaiser Wilhelm II's deformed hand. Thus the novel can be viewed from a political perspective as either a reactionary glorification of the monarchy or a comic send-up of royal pomp and circumstance among aristocrats who no longer fulfill any substantial political function. Klaus Heinrich's older brother Albrecht refuses to play along with what he derisively terms a "farce" (*Affentheater*) (p. 180), and the real solution to the duchy's economic problems comes from the profits of American monopoly capitalism.

Death in Venice

By the spring of 1911 it had been more than ten years since Thomas Mann had written the final lines of *Buddenbrooks*. He had become a famous writer, but he was still anxious to achieve more. "I am thirty years old now," he had written to Heinrich a few years earlier; "it is time to start thinking about a masterpiece" (December 5, 1905). Dismissing *Royal Highness* as "child's play," Mann mentioned the more ambitious plan to write a historical novel about Frederick the Great. Other unfinished projects included *Maja*, a social novel set in a modern metropolis conceived as the counterpart to the provincial world of *Buddenbrooks*, a novella inspired by Mann's hatred for the critic Theodor Lessing (*A Miserable Man*; *Ein Elender*), and the essay "Intellect and Art." In May, Mann decided that it was time for a vacation. Accompanied by Katia and Heinrich, he traveled south, spending the week of May 26 through June 2 in the luxurious Hotel des Bains on the Lido in Venice. Here a charming teenager caught Mann's eye (he was later identified as the Polish Baron Wladyslaw Moes). Back in Munich a month later Mann was already able to report in a letter of July 3 to Hans von Hülsen that he was at work on a "difficult if not impossible novella." The novella proved difficult indeed, as Mann agonized over it for a full year, but when it was finally published in the fall of 1912, it was immediately hailed as a modern classic.

The story is quickly told: the famous writer Gustav von Aschenbach is exhausted and decides that it is time for a vacation. He travels to Venice, where he takes a room in the Hotel des Bains. There Tadzio, a Polish teenager, attracts his attention. Although warned that he should leave Venice immediately because of a cholera outbreak, Aschenbach remains, enthralled by the boy's beauty until he collapses and dies. As the brief plot summary suggests, autobiographical parallels between Gustav von Aschenbach and his author are unmistakable. Katia Mann recalled that Mann incorporated other details from the vacation into his novella as well: the aging homosexual on the ship to Venice, the British clerk who warns Aschenbach to leave town, and the mildly obscene Neapolitan singer all had their real-life counterparts.[8] Of course, Mann did not die of cholera in Venice and the confessional aspects of the story are further complicated by characters drawn from other sources and deflected onto fictional masks. Gustav von Aschenbach's first name and his physical appearance are derived from the composer Gustav Mahler, who was a friend of the Pringsheim family. Katia's twin brother Klaus had worked for Mahler as an unpaid apprentice and Mann had been impressed by Mahler when they met in September 1910 at the premiere of his Eighth Symphony. He was shaken by Mahler's death on May 18, 1911 at the age of fifty. Goethe's influence was also important: Mann had originally considered a novella inspired by the seventy-year-old Goethe's love for the teenage Ulrike von Levetzow, an unrequited passion that inspired the late "Marienbad Elegies." Other Goethean models include *The Man of Fifty* (*Der Mann von fünfzig Jahren*), a novella about a father who falls in love with his son's fiancée, and *Elective Affinities* (*Die Wahlverwandtschaften*), a novel about marital infidelity and destructive passion that Mann said he read five times while writing *Death in Venice*. Philosophical influences include Plato's *Phaedrus* and *Symposium*, as well as Nietzsche's *Birth of Tragedy*.

The fact that Mann attributes authorship of his own uncompleted projects to Aschenbach nevertheless suggests an affinity between the author and his protagonist that goes deeper than the details of a trip to Venice or the eccentrics he encountered along the way. *Death in Venice* can in fact be read as a summation of Mann's early career, a final novella that rehearses one more time Mann's deepest preoccupations, while pointing the way toward a new interest in myth that will play an important role in his subsequent career. Like Tonio Kröger, Aschenbach inherits a combination of distinction and stigmatization from his parents: his father comes from a long line of respected civil servants and military officers, but his mother is the daughter of a bohemian musician who passes on to him the "darker, more fiery impulses" of the artist and "certain exotic racial characteristics in his external appearance."[9] Gustav von Aschenbach is also a representational writer, whose works reveal "a hidden affinity, indeed a congruence, between the personal destiny of the author and the wider destiny of his generation" (p. 202). Like Mann, Aschenbach writes works that appeal simultaneously to the intellectual elite and the general reading public. *Durchhalten* (hold fast, stay the course) is his favorite word (p. 201), referring to the discipline that drives him to "work on the brink of exhaustion" (p. 203). Finally, Gustav von Aschenbach succumbs to catastrophe like Little Herr Friedemann before him, as a visitation of repressed, destructive forces disrupts his precarious mental equilibrium and sends him spinning toward degradation and death.

The opening chapter of *Death in Venice* combines realistic detail with psychological depth and symbolic density in a way that sets the tone for the entire work. The writer leaves his apartment on Prinz-Regenten Strasse in Munich on an unseasonably warm afternoon in early May for a long walk. We follow him past the English Gardens to the edge of a cemetery, where he picks up a tram that takes him back to his apartment. Instead of being refreshed by his walk, however, Aschenbach returns home disturbed and convinced that he must leave town – and not just to his normal retreat in the country. A silent encounter with a strange man seems to be the source of his discomfort. While Aschenbach was waiting for the streetcar across from the cemetery, a man standing at the top of an open-air staircase suddenly caught his eye. The man returned Aschenbach's gaze with a startling directness. He was skinny, pale, and beardless, with red hair and a broad-brimmed hat that made him look foreign. Aschenbach had turned away and "forgotten" the man almost immediately, but then found himself entranced by a vivid daydream about a tropical landscape filled with lush plants, exotic birds, and tigers peering out of bamboo thickets. When he came to his senses and boarded the streetcar, the man had vanished.

Why is the man standing in the cemetery, and why does Aschenbach find his gaze so disturbing? A number of hints suggest that the encounter is sexual: the boldness of the man's stare and the implicit threat that he might "make an issue of the matter" (*die Sache aufs Äußerste zu treiben*) (p. 197) suggest that Aschenbach may have stumbled onto an urban site for clandestine homosexual rendezvous. The narrator's comment that the sight of the man "gave [Aschenbach's] thoughts an altogether different turn" (p. 196) may hint discreetly in this direction, as does Aschenbach's vigorous denial of the encounter's significance: "It was simply a desire to travel" (p. 197). In the larger context of the story, the man's appearance matches that of the pale, red-haired guitarist, "half pimp, half actor" (p. 249), who entertains the hotel guests in Venice with his lewdly ambiguous songs; in the still larger context of Mann's *oeuvre*, the man anticipates the devil in *Doctor Faustus*, who first appears as a red-haired pimp. The choice of Italy as a destination is also suggestive, as Italy was known as a site for sexual adventures as well as for tourism of a more edifying sort. "Here and there among a thousand other hawkers there are slyly whispering sales-men who invite you to follow them to 'very pretty' girls – and not only girls," Mann had written to his friend Otto Grautoff while visiting Naples as a young man (November 8, 1896). In *Death in Venice*, homosexual prostitution spreads north as the cholera epidemic worsens: "commercial vice now took on obtru-sive and extravagant forms which had hitherto been unknown in this area and indigenous only to southern Italy or oriental countries" (p. 254). Aschenbach's exchange of glances with the stranger in the cemetery thus awakens latent homosexual desires that send him on a journey south to the land of forbidden pleasures.

What distinguishes *Death in Venice* from Mann's earlier fiction and makes it a landmark achievement of European modernism is the way that Mann trans-ports a potentially sordid tale of sexual obsession into the realm of symbol and myth. On a realistic level, the strange man is probably a pimp, but he is also a symbol of death and a manifestation of the god Hermes. Aschenbach notices that the man's lips seem too short, exposing his teeth and gums in a way that is reminiscent of a skull – and he is standing in a cemetery, after all, in a story with "death" in its title and as its last word. The man's straw hat, walking stick, belted outfit, and crossed feet also identify him as Hermes in his guise as the guide of souls to the underworld, as many commentators have noticed, in the first of many allusions to Greek mythology in the text. The unlicensed gondo-lier who takes Aschenbach to his hotel in Venice in his black, coffin-like boat is also Charon, the mythical Greek ferryman who carries newly deceased souls across the river Styx to the House of Hades. Aschenbach calls Tadzio a "little Phaeacian" (p. 219), referring to the carefree people who host Odysseus on his way home from the Trojan War, and he has the head of Eros, the god of beauty and love. The sunrise is likened to the sun-god Helios driving his fiery chariot through the sky, and Aschenbach dreams of Dionysus, the Greek god of wine and sexual abandon.

The many critical commentaries to *Death in Venice* identify these and more classical allusions; what concerns us here is their significance for the work as a whole. Most obviously, the references to classical mythology elevate the work from the merely personal or specifically historical to the universal. The appreciation of beauty, the experience of sexual passion, and the knowledge of death's inevitability are common to all humans alive today or in the past. Classical mythology provides a timeless vocabulary to express eternal truths of the human condition. At the same time, one could also argue that Mann's linking of lust, disease, artistic creativity, and death are not universal, but the product of a specific historical constellation of ideas that leads back through the work of Nietzsche, Wagner, and Schopenhauer to German romanticism. From this perspective, *Death in Venice* does not reveal eternal truths after all, but only a specific nineteenth-century pessimistic philosophy. What unites Schopenhauer and Nietzsche and distinguishes them from Hegel and Marx is their opposition to notions of historical progress or human development. Beneath the changing forms of this world lies only the amoral force of the will, the inchoate desires of the Dionysian realm. Mann harnesses the seemingly timeless vocabulary of classical antiquity to express a time-bound philosophy in opposition to both Enlightenment optimism and socialist activism.

Myth in *Death in Venice* also serves as camouflage, as a strategy of conceal-ment rather than revelation. In its own way, the content of *Death in Venice* is as controversial as that of Vladimir Nabokov's *Lolita*: Nabokov writes of a middle-aged man's desire for a twelve-year-old girl; in Mann's case, the object of desire is a fourteen-year-old boy. *Death in Venice* is about homosexuality, stalking, and pedophilia, topics that were as explosive then as they are now. Just a few years before Mann wrote *Death in Venice*, the journalist Maximilian Harden had written a series of articles in which he contended that Prince Philipp of Eulenburg, a confidant of Kaiser Wilhelm II, was a homosexual. The articles sparked public controversy and a series of lawsuits that eventually confirmed Harden's allegations, but which made him unpopular and caused a precipitous drop in sales of his journal. Harden was a friend of Hedwig Pringsheim, Mann's mother-in-law, and Mann sided with him against Eulenburg in the dispute. Mann's biographer Hermann Kurzke has argued that the fact that Mann supported the Jewish Harden proves that he was not an anti-Semite,[10] which may be the case, but under the circumstances, the closeted Mann had little choice but to side with the friend of his mother-in-law who had publicly denounced a homosexual. Mann's public identity as a "respectable" writer and paterfamilias was based, after all, on the assumption that he was solidly hetero-sexual in his desires. But now he was writing what could easily be interpreted as an indirect confession of his homosexuality. No wonder that Mann described his new project as "difficult, if not impossible"! "It is about an aging artist's love for a boy," he wrote to Philipp Witkop; "you say 'my, my!' but it is very respect-able" (July 18, 1911). Casting Aschenbach's forbidden passion as an example of "Greek love" gave the otherwise scandalous topic an aura of respectability: the story is about artistic inspiration and Platonic philosophy, Mann could argue, not about homosexuality and certainly not about me! And besides, nothing hap-pens. Aschenbach does not seduce Tadzio; he writes an essay instead.

Upon closer reading, however, precisely this use of classical myth as cam-ouflage is exposed as a deception in the course of *Death in Venice*. As noted, Aschenbach's first conscious reaction to the troubling encounter with the man in the cemetery is to deny its significance, insisting to himself that his sudden vision of a seething swamp is just a symptom of a normal desire to take a vacation. His early encounters with Tadzio reveal a similar desire to disarm visceral desire with irony and classical allusions: "Good, good!" remarks Aschenbach as he gazes for the first time at Tadzio "with that cool professional approval in which artists confronted by a masterpiece sometimes cloak their ecstasy, their rapture" (p. 220). He is tempted to wag his finger at Tadzio when he watches him kiss another boy and smiles as he thinks of the ancient Greek Critobulus, who had stolen a kiss from the son of Alcibiades. As Aschenbach becomes increasingly obsessed with Tadzio, however, his efforts to sublimate passion into references to Greek mythology become ineffective. Conscious allusions yield to unconscious desires; wry references to antiquity give way to riotous dreams of Dionysian passion. On the ship to Venice, Aschenbach had observed with disgust an elderly man who had dolled himself up to mix with his young companions; now he visits the hotel barber daily and begins dyeing his hair and wearing make-up to attract the boy. The ironic masks that were a sign of intellectual distance and emotional discipline now become a sign of his degradation, his loss of control.

The exposure of the mask as a mask and thus a lie comes to a head shortly before Aschenbach's death. The author who had once so sternly denounced "gypsies" and their bohemian sympathy with the abyss now realizes that his moralizing pose was hypocritical. The source of his artistic inspiration is passion, base lust, and thus any attempt to elevate the writer into a moral model for the people is a ridiculous endeavor that should be forbidden. Here Mann moves far beyond the melancholy observations of Tonio Kröger, who confesses a slightly sentimental love for the bourgeois normalcy he cannot enjoy. Aschenbach claims that the inspiring force of his art is an uncontrollable desire for sexual debauchery. In a daring move, Mann simultaneously elevates his story of homosexual passion into a timeless classical myth and exposes that myth-making process as a subterfuge designed to conceal the truth. He writes a textbook example of classical art that simultaneously demonstrates why such art should not be included in student textbooks.

Death in Venice can therefore be read as a masked confession, a timeless myth, an expression of nineteenth-century philosophical pessimism, and as a modernist exposé of mendacious mythopoeia. Still other aspects of the novella link it directly to its historical setting. We are told in the opening sentence that the story takes place in an unspecified year of the new twentieth century. *Death in Venice* includes references to modern technologies such as motor busses, telephones, and steam ships; it ends with the mysterious image of a deserted camera on the beach. To be sure, the precise date and the nature of the threats to Europe mentioned in the opening sentence are left vague; what matters is not a specific event, but a general sense of crisis. That crisis is registered in terms of the mentality that Edward Said describes as "Orientalist."[11] *Death in Venice* takes place at a time when the vast majority of the world was under the direct or indirect control of European imperial powers. As Said argues, the actual physical control of the European colonies was buttressed by an Orientalist ideology that posited Western superiority and thereby legitimated the European exploitation of non-European regions.

Death in Venice unfolds within the symbolic landscape of the imperial era and also reflects a crisis of confidence in the ideology that supports it. The cholera that kills Aschenbach originates in India and has spread throughout Asia before it reaches Venice. From the opening pages of the novella, Aschenbach's crisis – defined multiply in terms of homosexuality, disease, and the Dionysian realm of uncontrolled passion – is also linked to the East. Aschenbach sees the stranger in the cemetery while he is studying the inscriptions on a building in Byzantine style that is decorated with Greek crosses and religious plaques, an edifice that anticipates the Oriental splendor of the San Marcos cathedral in Venice. He dreams immediately of jungles and tigers, and the images recur in his vivid dream shortly before he dies. The association of the East with barbarism goes back to antiquity; one of Mann's sources for *Death in Venice* was Euripides' *Bacchae*, which draws on the myth that Dionysus came to Europe from India. At the same time, *Death in Venice* may also reflect the findings of modern science, for it was written shortly after Robert Koch was making his pioneering discoveries in bacteriology. As recent cultural historians have shown, the language of infectious disease was frequently grafted on to colonialist rhetoric that described the non-European peoples as foreign bodies that threatened to contaminate their colonial masters.[12]

Gustav von Aschenbach is a representative writer, but not so much a representative of the German nation as a representative of Europe. We are told in the opening chapter that he is "too preoccupied with the tasks imposed upon him by his own sensibility and the collective European psyche" to travel extensively, and that "he had never even been tempted to venture outside Europe" (p. 198). But he does not need to leave Europe, for "Asia" comes to him, not only in the form of the cholera that causes his death, but also in the seeds of chaos that lie beneath his cultivated exterior. As Sigmund Freud famously remarked, the human subconscious is like a "dark continent." The threat to the civilized order that Europeans projected on to the native peoples of their colonial outposts was also present at home in the form of the illicit desires and unconscious impulses that Mann ironically termed the "dogs in the basement." *Death in Venice* is not only about the incursion of destructive forces into

Europe from the East, but also about the upwelling of repressed desires from within. The events of the novella take place in locations that mark the threshold between two worlds: Venice is part of Europe, but its Arabian-style arches and Byzantine cathedral also mark it as the gateway to the Orient. Aschenbach sees the stranger in a deserted cemetery, a location that is part of the city and yet set apart from it. He is from Silesia, on the German-Polish border, and he is therefore able to make out Tadzio's name "with the help of a few Polish memories." Mann's identification of Eastern Europe and Russia as an "Asiatic" realm will continue in *The Magic Mountain* and *Doctor Faustus*; already in *Death in Venice*, Tadzio is a liminal figure who stands on the border of Europe and Asia, the embodiment of Greek perfection, but also the gateway to the destructive Dionysian forces of the East.

In his essay on "Lübeck as a Spiritual Form of Life," Mann describes the affinity between his own city-state of Lübeck and Venice, which he sees as symbolized in the almond-paste candy called marzipan. He speculates that this local specialty of Lübeck originated in an Oriental harem and came north to Lübeck by way of Venice. He goes on to describe himself as a kind of marzipan, a mixture of East and West (or North and South), with his Hanseatic father and his mother from Brazil, and contends further "that *Death in Venice* is really 'marzipan,'" in its mixture of the alien with the familiar. With remarkable density, the novella is about a crisis of heterosexual masculinity told in terms of nineteenth-century philosophical pessimism elevated to the realm of classical mythology. It develops a theory of artistic creativity in the vocabulary of Platonic philosophy, while it is at the same time a work of disguised autobiography. Finally, it reflects not just a crisis of individual creativity or sexual identity, but also a crisis of European confidence at the height of the imperial era and on the eve of the First World War.

East = Dionysian

Chapter 4

From world war to the Weimar Republic

Mann's wartime journalism

Thomas Mann was in his summer home in Bad Tölz when war broke out in the summer of 1914. Although no one knew at that point how long the war would last or how devastating its effects would be, Mann quickly sensed that it was a life-changing event. "What a fateful blow!" wrote Mann to Heinrich on August 7, 1914. He wondered what Europe would look like when it was all over, but for the time being expressed his "deepest sympathy with Germany," not realizing that his brother felt rather differently. Heinrich had just completed *Man of Straw* (*Der Untertan*), a devastating satire of the German Kaiserreich that the publisher hastily withdrew from circulation until the end of the war. Heinrich Mann nevertheless soon emerged as one of the few German intellectuals who did not share in the patriotic fervor that swept the nation in August 1914. His brother, Thomas, in contrast, stood firmly with the majority in his initial enthusiasm for the war.

Mann was already thirty-nine years old at the beginning of the First World War and until this time he had been what he termed "a nonpolitical man." While his father had been a high-ranking official in the local government of Lübeck, Mann seemed content to focus his energies on his art and to leave the business of government to those in charge. When called upon, Mann fulfilled his civic duty: he reported promptly when drafted into the army in 1900, although he was happy to accept the medical discharge for flat feet that his mother helped engineer with a compliant doctor a few months later. He also worked as a literary censor for the Bavarian government before the war, where he proved liberal in his taste – for instance, Mann argued that Frank Wedekind's shocking depictions of adolescent sexuality should be permitted, even while making no secret of his distaste for the man – but there is no indication that he was opposed to the notion of government censorship per se. His literary works certainly revealed no socialist sympathies: Consul Buddenbrook makes the angry mob look foolish in the 1848 Revolution, and if the aristocrats in *Royal Highness* are portrayed as mildly eccentric and ineffectual rulers, they are nothing like the pompous blowhards in *Man of Straw* – and in any case, as Mann insisted, the novel was really about the plight of the artist.

Beginning in August 1914, however, Mann began to write a series of political essays defending Germany's entry into the war. "Thoughts in War" ("Gedanken im Krieg," 1914) hailed the conflict as a "purification, liberation, and source of hope" for a nation that was suddenly unified and radically determined. To be sure, Mann's defense of the war effort was couched more in terms of Nietzsche's philosophy than military strategy. In *The Birth of Tragedy*, Nietzsche argues that the "noble simplicity and quiet grandeur" that Johann Winckelmann had admired in ancient Greek sculpture was merely the outward "Apollinian" form of dark and powerful "Dionysian" forces. According to Nietzsche, Socrates brought an end to Greek tragedy by reducing the incommensurable to mere irony. In Mann's adaptation of this logic, German culture (*Kultur*) is the genuine expression of the Dionysian forces released by the war, whereas French civilization (*Zivilisation*) is only superficial rationality. German culture is manly, filled with tragic-heroic resolution; French civilization is effeminate and hypocritical: "they are just like suffragettes," writes Mann – first they throw bombs to provoke a conflict and then they cry foul in a high falsetto when the enemy strikes back. Mann turned next to an essay on Frederick the Great, transforming what he had originally planned as a historical novel into a character study of the German leader. Mann makes no effort to portray Frederick as an appealing or likeable individual, but in his reckless aggression, his ascetic commitment to duty, and his hatred of women he allowed himself to be used as an instrument of fate that guided the Prussian army to victory. In a third essay written in the form of a letter to a Swedish newspaper, Mann again expressed his nationalist pride, his disdain for the French, and his outrage that they would dare to deploy black Senegalese troops from the French colonies along the German border – "an animal with lips as thick as pillows."

Mann's early wartime journalism reveals him at his most unpleasant: a jingoistic nationalist seething with hatred that he expressed in misogynist and racist terms. What provoked Mann to take such a hard-line stance in support of the German war effort? To begin with, Mann's vitriolic statements were not unusual in the context of the times; as suggested, it was Heinrich who was out of step with the majority opinion. The war also provided Mann with an opportunity to realize his long-held ambition to be an intellectual leader of the German nation. On a psychological level, Mann's ridicule of the effeminate French in the name of a manly German nationalism allowed him to proclaim in public that he was "one of the boys" – in spirit, of course, as doctors quickly excused Mann from the call to active duty that befell many men his age and older – thus repressing nagging doubts about his sexual orientation. Finally, the war allowed Mann to turn long-simmering tensions with his brother Heinrich into open conflict.

In November 1915 Heinrich published an essay titled "Zola" about the French novelist who had championed the cause of Alfred Dreyfus, a Jewish soldier falsely accused of spying by a right-wing government that refused to admit its mistake. The essay was a thinly veiled attack in the name of French intellect and democracy on the current German leaders, but Thomas Mann understood the statement that "the intellectual fellow-travelers (*Mitläufer*) are even guiltier than those in power" as a direct personal rebuke. For the better part of the next two years, Mann devoted himself to the *Reflections of a Nonpolitical Man (Betrachtungen eines Unpolitischen*, 1918). It began as an assault on Heinrich and the liberalism he represented (although Mann never explicitly names Heinrich in the *Reflections*), but evolved into a brooding assessment of his own political opinions and a look back at the first half of his career. As Klaus Mann recalled, this was not a happy time for his father, who took to wearing a drab, quasi-military tunic, went for days and weeks without shaving, and had a look of grim suffering about him.[1] Mann broke off all personal contact with his brother – although he continued to read and respond indirectly in the *Reflections* to everything that Heinrich published – and became close friends with Ernst Bertram, a conservative intellectual who was working on a book about Nietzsche and whose partner, Ernst Glöckner, was associated with Stefan George's circle of admirers.

Mann begins the *Reflections* with a description of Germany as the Reich that refuses to be assimilated into the West. Mann equates Western civilization with literature, intellect, the French Revolution, and imperialism; Germany with music, spirituality, conservatism, and cosmopolitanism. Mann's enemies are France, the French allies of the Entente, including Britain and Russia (although Mann later argues that the Russian alliance with the West is actually a misalliance, as Russian spirituality renders them closer in spirit to the Germans), and of course Heinrich. Very quickly, however, Mann begins to complicate the seemingly clear distinctions between Germany and France, and between Heinrich and himself. There are in fact two Germanies, Mann contends, in an argument that reproduces the distinction between Lübeck and Berlin that he had drawn in *Buddenbrooks*. The politically disengaged burghers of the old German city-state have spiritual depth and a cosmopolitan openness to the world, whereas the capitalist bourgeoisie of the new national capital have absorbed the militant nationalism and imperialist ambitions of the West. Mann's critique of France is therefore also a polemic against what he terms the "de-Germanification of Germany." Almost from the outset, however, Mann is aware that his effort to "keep Germany German" is doomed to failure. He is fighting a defensive battle against the tide of history – but he is also fighting a battle against himself. For all his praise of German music and spirituality, Mann knows that he is as much a literary man as is his brother, that he is waging war against rhetoric and intellect with the very weapons that he condemns. As a result of this self-consciousness, Mann repeatedly undermines his own arguments in the *Reflections*, lending introspective depth – if at the expense of logical coherence – to what otherwise would have been a tediously repetitious polemic.

Of particular interest is Mann's critique of imperialism and his defense of an alternate German tradition that hovers between Goethean cosmopolitanism and *völkisch* nationalism. As Mann argues, the French Revolution in the name of universal human rights led inevitably, if paradoxically, to imperialism and racism. Convinced that their path to democracy was based on values that should be common to all, the French (and also the British) felt it their right and duty to export their civilization to the rest of the world. The result of this arrogant endeavor, as Mann views it, was to eradicate distinct national identities in the name of supposedly universal values. Those who do not share enlightened European beliefs are little more than benighted barbarians, and thus the British in India preach universal rights but practice racial discrimination, and the same is true of slave-owning Americans or the French who invaded Morocco.

Against what he perceives as the hypocrisy of Western civilization, Mann defines an alternative tradition of German culture. Mann begins by confessing that he is not a "proper German," because he has absorbed intellectual influences from multiple European cultures and because he has inherited some of his mother's Latin-American "blood-mixture." Mann goes on to argue that Schopenhauer, Nietzsche, and Wagner were also as much European as they were German, and that such openness to the world is a typically German virtue. Luther resisted Roman Catholicism in the name of individual spiritual development that was more suited to the German temperament; Goethe preferred organic evolution to the violence of French Revolution; Nietzsche regarded with skepticism the growing militancy of Bismarck's Germany. Looking back at his own development, Mann argues that because he grew up in Lübeck and lives in Munich rather than Berlin, he has "slept a little through the metamorphosis of the German burgher into the bourgeois."[2]

Thus far Mann's argument in the *Reflections* seems appealing enough, pitting as it does German humanism and cosmopolitanism against the racist imperialism of Western civilization. Unfortunately, however, it also contains elements of the *völkisch* nationalism mentioned earlier. In theory, at least, anyone can become a French or American citizen, regardless of their place of birth or ethnic background. *Völkisch* nationalists, in contrast, limited membership in the nation to those who shared a common ethnicity or race. One of Mann's primary influences in this regard was Paul de Lagarde, an anti-democratic, anti-Semitic conservative who celebrated the mystical unity of the German *Volk*. Mann hails Lagarde as a *praeceptor Germaniae* in the *Reflections* and cites him frequently; he also quotes surreptitiously from the work of Houston Stewart Chamberlain, although he is never explicitly identified. To his credit, Mann avoids the blatant anti-Semitism of these writers in *Reflections*, reserving his venom for what he terms "civilization's literary man" – although elsewhere Mann describes as "typically Jewish" the piercing intellect and linguistic facility that he attributes in the *Reflections* to the *Zivilisationsliterat*. Mann's proud identification of his own mixed heritage is also at odds with the stress on ethnic "purity" among *völkisch* nationalists, and he would go on to oppose the racist ideology of National Socialism. That he would cite such authors as Lagarde and Chamberlain with approval in the *Reflections* is disturbing, but also a reminder that not all those who indulged in proto-fascist ideas became supporters of Nazi Germany. Ernst Bertram, Mann's closest friend at the time, did; Mann did not.

The evolution of Mann's political thought

Just four years after the publication of the *Reflections of a Nonpolitical Man*, Mann astonished his contemporaries by delivering an impassioned speech in support of the beleaguered Weimar Republic. "The German Republic" ("Von deutscher Republik," 1922) presents the former enemy of democracy as its friend and ally – while at the same time Mann insisted that he had not changed at all, or at least not in any fundamental way. Why did Mann's political thought evolve toward support of the Weimar Republic, and to what extent are his ideas consistent with his earlier point of view?

We are unusually well-informed about Mann's intellectual development between the years 1918 and 1921 because he preserved his diaries of those years (they were the only pre-1933 diaries that he did not burn in the 1940s, presumably because he needed them as source material for *Doctor Faustus*). By any measure, these were tumultuous years: Germany lost the war, the Kaiser abdicated, and Munich was ruled briefly by a communist government that was brutally ousted by right-wing paramilitary forces. Mann followed these developments closely and while his reactions to specific individuals and events fluctuated, his political thought gradually coalesced around the idea that Germany needed to pursue a third way, a form of government that was in keeping with its national identity as the "land of the center" between Eastern and Western Europe. Mann sometimes referred to his goal as a "third Reich" (long before the term became associated with Nazi Germany); elsewhere he spoke of the need for a "conservative revolution."[3]

The specific event that prompted Mann to write "The German Repub-lic" was the assassination of German Foreign Minister Walter Rathenau on June 24, 1922 by ultra-nationalist zealots. Mann urges a skeptical audience of right-wing students to overcome their hostility to democracy and to throw their support behind the Republic. Mann insists that he has not renounced the conservative principles behind the *Reflections*, but that his thought has evolved organically in response to a changing situation. Twice he reassures his audience that the Republic that he supports is not to be confused with some-thing for "clever Jewish boys" (*scharfe Judenjungen*) – an anti-Semitic aside that pandered to the audience's prejudices, but that was particularly ironic, given that Rathenau was a Jew. A year earlier Mann had written an essay on the "Jewish Question" ("Zur jüdischen Frage," 1921) in which he explained that while he was not a Jew, as some had assumed, he was also no anti-Semite. Mann finds it shameful that university students in Munich rejected a profes-sor simply because he was Jewish and insists that he has no sympathy for the current "swastika nonsense" (*Hakenkreuzunfug*) – thus making Mann one of the first German intellectuals to condemn the nascent fascist movement. At the same time, Mann cites with apparent approval Goethe's comment that the Jews "were never worth much as a people" and adds that there is something unpleasant and even dangerous about them. Perhaps not surprisingly, Katia was upset when Mann read her the essay aloud and insisted that he withdraw it from publication, which he did.

As so often, Mann's comments seem designed to please no one: just when he has made an unequivocal declaration of his philo-Semitism, he makes remarks that are difficult to interpret as anything but anti-Semitic. The logic behind these seemingly contradictory comments is roughly as follows: the Jews are a distinct ethnic group (Mann fluctuates between definitions of that difference in terms of biological race and cultural behavior). Jewish intellectuals have a facility with language and a biting wit that Mann sometimes finds irritat-ing, but that he frequently welcomes as a necessary corrective to the German tendency toward melancholy and music. Mann's ambivalent attitude toward the Jews is further complicated by his awareness that he shares many of the characteristics that he identifies as "typically Jewish." Although Mann rejects early German fascism in no uncertain terms, he continues to indulge in the sort of Jewish stereotypes that appear in his earliest fiction, despite the growing power of more virulent forms of anti-Semitism. In fact, at this point in his career he actively denied the growing menace. In 1921, Jakob Wassermann sent Mann a copy of his autobiography, *My Path as a German and a Jew* (*Mein Weg als Deutscher und Jude*), in which he complained that he had been the victim of prejudice. Mann dismissed Wassermann's comments as "nonsense" and symptoms of "poetic hypochondria," while insisting that anti-Semitism could never take root in cosmopolitan Germany.[4] Wassermann responded angrily: "You are celebrated for your Hanseatic heritage, I am hated as a Jew, and you cannot understand or perceive my suffering."

In his effort to defend what he argues is a specifically German form of democracy, Mann enlists two unlikely allies: the German romantic poet Friedrich von Hardenberg, better known by his penname, Novalis, and the American Walt Whitman. At first glance, Novalis hardly seems qualified as a proponent of democracy: his aphorism collection "Faith and Love" ("Glauben und Liebe," 1798) celebrates the newly crowned Prussian king and queen, while the essay "Christianity or Europe" ("Die Christenheit oder Europa," 1799) evokes a nostalgic image of the Middle Ages. Mann nevertheless insists that this seeming reactionary is actually a radical Jacobin in disguise – a reading of Novalis that was highly unorthodox at the time but has been supported by more recent Novalis scholars.[5] Whitman's credentials as a singer of democracy are unquestioned, but the American's status as an advocate of an intrinsically German republic would seem to be in doubt. What unites the two – in Mann's mind at least – is their common commitment to a form of democracy based on erotic bonds between men. Mann had read with great interest Hans Blüher's *The Role of Eroticism in Male Society* (*Die Rolle der Erotik in der männlichen Gesellschaft*, 1917–19), in which Blüher argues that male–male eroticism is the glue that binds society together in rigid discipline. Men who devote their attention to their wives and children are effeminate, inferior, and typically Jewish. Mann adopts the central tenant of Blüher's work, but adapts it to his purposes, turning a misogynist and anti-Semitic defense of an authoritarian society into a call for a homoerotically charged German democracy.

Many have found Mann's arguments confusing and unconvincing, a point of view that Mann did little to refute in private. "I don't take intellectual arguments too seriously," he wrote to Bertram on December 25, 1922; "are not 'thoughts' for the artist only dialectical means to an end that is useful for life?" The intellectual means of "The German Republic" may be questionable, but the end is clearly in support of the Weimar Republic. Whether or not Mann's thought was consistent with the *Reflections*, as he was so anxious to claim in public, is ultimately less important than the fact that he came down early and firmly on the right side of history in his support of German democracy and his rejection of National Socialism. In the course of eight years, Mann had come a long way: from the "nonpolitical" writer who welcomed the outbreak of the First World War to the inveterate newspaper reader and political essayist that he remained for the rest of his career.

A return to literature

Two days after completing the *Reflections of a Nonpolitical Man* in March 1918, Thomas Mann began writing a detailed description of his dog, Bauschan. *A Man and his Dog (Herr und Hund,* 1919) would occupy Mann until the following October, swelling to nearly one hundred pages. The work is subtitled "an idyll," a genre with roots in antiquity that enjoyed a renaissance in eighteenth-century German literature. The idyll is defined both by what it is and what it is not: a charming description of a bucolic scene that deliberately avoids historical reality. As would be the case with his Joseph novels during the years of exile, *A Man and his Dog* provided Mann with a refuge from political events and a break from his years of wartime journalism. He also viewed it as a kind of warm-up exercise, a way of limbering up his creative powers before attempting to complete *The Magic Mountain.*

Although it was not intended as a major work, *A Man and his Dog* is nevertheless interesting on a number of levels. It is an intimately, if selectively, autobiographical text, focusing at length on Mann's afternoon walks and his relationship with his dog, while bracketing out problematic aspects of his life and contemporary events. Mann was a dog lover and owner throughout his life; *A Man and his Dog* radiates with gratitude for the simple pleasure afforded him by a daily walk with his loyal friend. The work is also a worthy addition to a literary tradition that extends from Cervantes' *Dialogue of the Dogs* through Kafka's *Investigations of a Dog* to Günter Grass' *Dog Years.* The long story also shows Mann's powers of observation and description at their height. While he is more famous for his depictions of human subjects, Mann focuses here on the riparian landscape near his Munich villa and the habits and moods of his canine companion. Mann's characterization of Bauschan fluctuates between playful personification and fascination with his distinctly animal instincts: he contrasts the healthy mutt of the common people with the neurotic, "aristocratic" purebred collie that he had portrayed in *Royal Highness.* Bauschan "smiles" and "laughs," but he also snuffles the private parts of other dogs and eats a live mouse whole. Perhaps most interesting from the perspective of today's interest in animal rights and the sometimes ridiculed movement to redefine pet ownership as companionship is Mann's focus on the symbiotic relationship between man and animal. He describes how the adopted pet gradually bonds with his master, how a protracted stay at the clinic drives the dog into a deep depression, and how the despondent animal reestablishes trust with his inscrutable overlord. The work that Mann referred to as his "dog story" (in English) was popular in translation as well as in German, and Mann frequently read passages from it during his public performances.

Mann was still not ready to resume work on his novel as the war came to an end, so he turned to another idyll, the *Song of the Little Child* (*Gesang vom Kindchen*, 1919). Mann wrote the poem in honor of new daughter, Elisabeth, born April 24, 1918. It describes her birth and baptism in the deliberately archaic verse-form of the hexameter, making it Mann's only mature work of poetry. There are several reasons why Mann made the peculiar decision to compose an old-fashioned verse epic in the midst of an increasingly desperate historical situation. One was that in terms of form and content it was as far away as possible from present concerns. Another was that it allowed him to weigh in against an old charge that he was a mere writer of prose fiction (*Schriftsteller*) and not an inspired poet (*Dichter*). There was a deep-seated prejudice in Germany against the novel as an inferior art form that still cast a long shadow in the early twentieth century, which was also one of the reasons that Mann had tried his hand at a drama. In addition, Mann continued to struggle against the impression that he lacked emotional warmth, just as in later life he bridled at the suggestion that his fiction was ponderously Teutonic. What better opportunity to prove his critics wrong than to write a heartfelt poem about his new baby girl? Finally, the verse epic gave Mann an opportunity to emulate Goethe, whose *Hermann und Dorothea* was also written as a celebration of domesticity in a time of war. Goethe's work was hailed as a minor classic by conservative nineteenth-century Germans and frequently included as required reading in schools, which was certainly another reason that Mann paid homage to Goethe in his own epic poem – even though Gustav von Aschenbach had made fun of deluded schoolteachers who used literature inspired by base desires to mold the tender minds of their students!

Although the *Song of the Little Child* is no masterpiece, marred as it is by awkward language and clumsy verse forms, it is interesting from a biographical perspective. Mann made no secret of the fact that he liked some of his children better than others. Elisabeth could do no wrong; her younger brother, Michael, born April 21, 1919, could do little right; Erika and Klaus were generally in his favor, Golo and Monika more often out. The *Song of the Little Child* also bears witness to Mann's tendency to play up the exoticism in his family background. Katia appears in the poem as a "fairy-tale bride," whose dark hair makes it seem as if she had come from the banks of the Nile. Elisabeth is said to have the blue eyes of her Hanseatic forefathers, but also "a little Oriental nose." As in the case of Imma Spoelmann's "shimmering blood mixture" in *Royal Highness*, Mann transforms the source of potential stigmatization – the Jewish origins of the Pringsheim family and thus also, in part, of his own children – into charmingly exotic signs of distinction.

The Magic Mountain

On Easter Sunday, April 1919, Mann finally resumed work on *The Magic Mountain*. The project dated back to 1912, when Katia was diagnosed – falsely, as it turned out – with tuberculosis. In the days before penicillin the only known treatment for the disease was to send patients to a sanatorium somewhere with clean air, usually in the mountains or the desert. Katia was sent to an Alpine sanatorium in Davos, Switzerland, where she stayed, with interruptions, for a total of almost a year between March 1912 and May 1914. Mann visited her there for three weeks in May and June 1912, and soon had an idea for a new novella, tentatively titled *The Enchanted Mountain* (*Der verzauberte Berg*). It was to be a short comic counterpart to *Death in Venice*. He worked intermittently on the project between 1912 and 1915, until the *Reflections of a Nonpolitical Man* began to absorb all his energy. By the time Mann began writing again, it had become clear to him that the originally conceived novella was becoming a major novel. More than five years would pass before Mann completed *The Magic Mountain* on September 27, 1924. For the third time in his career, Mann had written a masterpiece, a work that together with *Buddenbrooks* and *Death in Venice* solidi-fied his status as one of Germany's most important living writers.

Although *The Magic Mountain* is a novel of monumental proportions, its plot can be summarized in a few sentences: Hans Castorp, a young man from Hamburg who is about to begin a career as a ship's engineer, travels south to visit his cousin Joachim Ziemssen, who is being treated for tuberculosis in a sanatorium in Davos, Switzerland. Soon after his arrival the chief doctor, Behrens, detects a suspicious spot on Castorp's lung and recommends that he extend his planned three-week vacation to an indefinite stay. Seven years pass by, and it is only the outbreak of the First World War that finally sends Castorp down from the mountain and onto the battlefield. Castorp has long since lost contact with his few remaining relatives in the "flatlands" and forgotten his career plans, but he has experienced and learned many things. He falls in love with a Russian woman, Clavdia Chauchat, and is introduced to new ideas by a series of mentor figures: Ludovico Settembrini, an Italian humanist and representative of the Enlightenment; Leo Naphta, an eastern European Jew raised by Jesuits who preaches an unusual combination of communism and catholicism; and Mynheer Peeperkorn, a malarial, alcoholic, incoherent, and impotent Dutch plantation owner from the East Indies with a mysteriously commanding presence.

In a lecture delivered to students at Princeton University in 1938, Mann argued that *The Magic Mountain* was a *Bildungsroman* (novel of education), which he viewed as a specifically German form of the novel that arose out of a combination of eighteenth-century religious autobiographies and the picaresque novel. Goethe provided the literary model for the genre with *Wilhelm Meister's Apprenticeship* (*Wilhelm Meisters Lehrjahre*, 1795), a novel about a young man who falls in with a troupe of not entirely respectable actors, but who eventually marries and plans to begin a career as a doctor. Goethe's *Wilhelm Meister* set the pattern for a series of nineteenth-century German novels in which – to paraphrase Hegel's sarcastic description of the genre – the hero typically sows a few wild oats before settling down to a job and a wife. The description hardly seems adequate for Hans Castorp, however, as he quickly forgets his career and has an affair with a married woman who leaves the sanatorium the next morning and returns in the company of another man. Thus critics have often wondered about the adequacy of Mann's description of *The Magic Mountain* as a *Bildungsroman*: to many, it has seemed more of a parody or inversion of the genre; others insist that Castorp experiences and learns enough to qualify Mann's work as a *Bildungsroman*, even if it lacks the usual happy ending that promises personal fulfillment and commitment to the community on the part of the protagonist.

Mann begins with a preface that sets the date of the events that are about to unfold in a past that is recent and yet infinitely removed from the present. The First World War was perceived as a radical break in the continuity of history for those who lived through it; everything that had happened before the conflict belonged to what Stefan Zweig famously termed "the world of yesterday" in his autobiography (*Die Welt von gestern*, 1942). Hans Castorp spends seven years on the mountain, which means that he arrives in the summer of 1907; he celebrates his thirtieth birthday just before the outbreak of the war, so he is twenty-three as the novel begins. As the narrator tells us, Castorp is an average individual, mediocre in a positive sense of the term, and for this reason he is also representative, a typical young German of the immediate prewar period. The fact that he is thirty when he heads out into the world can be read as an ironic allusion to Jesus Christ, who is said to have been about the same age when he began his ministry (Luke, 3:23). Oskar Matzerath, the hero of Günter

Grass' *Tin Drum*, also turns thirty at the end of the novel, and Grass makes explicit the parallels between Jesus and Oskar as a representative German of the next generation. Mann's preface also introduces us to the narrator, who emerges as a character in his own right: at various times chatty, avuncular, and philosophical, he styles himself as an old-fashioned storyteller, "that conjuror who murmurs in past tenses."[6] The narrative voice is part of Mann's old strategy of the "double optic": he tells us to sit back and relax for a good long read (because only that which is told in detail is genuinely entertaining), and we follow "our hero" with sympathy, amusement, and concern. At the same time, *The Magic Mountain* will belie its realistic veneer by including lengthy philosophical speculations and political debates, while making allusions to ancient myth and modern psychology.

The Magic Mountain begins *in medias res*, with Hans Castorp's arrival at the sanatorium. Chapter two is a flashback to his childhood and youth, and the rest of the novel unfolds chronologically. As Katia Mann later recalled, many of the characters in the novel were based directly on individuals whom Mann observed during his three-week stay in Davos; their daily routine of heavy meals followed by rest on the freezing balcony while wrapped in blankets and frequent temperature measurements also corresponds to life in the Davos sanatorium.[7] The descriptions were so close to life, in fact, that some of the doctors complained that they had been slandered by their depiction in the novel, joining a long list of individuals who recognized themselves in unflattering portraits in Mann's fiction. The mood in the opening chapter hovers between the giddy and the macabre. Castorp greets his cousin Joachim Ziemssen with the shy reserve of a young man from northern Europe who has been taught to keep his feelings under control – later he will blush uncontrollably when Joachim dares to call him by his first name – but he soon finds himself laughing hilariously about the dead bodies that are discreetly removed from the sanatorium at night in bobsleds. The incident is an early warning that the normal rules of social decorum do not apply on the mountain. Castorp is a fastidious dresser with impeccable table manners, to be sure, but he will be awakened the next morning to the sounds of neighbors having sex in the room next door.

Death and sex permeate the atmosphere at the sanatorium. Although the patients ostensibly come to be cured, many know that they are coming to die; in the case of Hans Castorp, a few days at the sanatorium turn a seemingly healthy young man into a chronic invalid. Between the frequent feedings and long naps there is little to do but flirt and gossip, and Castorp soon develops a crush on Clavdia Chauchat and is initiated into the petty jealousies and rivalries between his fellow patients. But Castorp also discovers hitherto unknown intellectual interests. The otherwise torpid young man, who enjoys dozing after a morning beer and cigarette, finds himself reading voraciously in biological textbooks and medieval treatises, while pondering weighty questions of time and eternity. To say that Castorp becomes a genius, as maintained by Hermann Weigand, an early and otherwise perceptive reader of *The Magic Mountain*, seems something of an exaggeration, but the sanatorium certainly stimulates his mind as well as his libido.[8]

The idea that sex, death, and genius are related to one another has its roots in German romanticism, although Mann draws on Nietzsche and Schopenhauer as well. Sexual intercourse involves a loss of individuality through the physical merging of two bodies and the mental surrender to irrational passion, but it can also lead to the creation of new life and serve as a metaphor for the creative genius released when the normal constraints of mental discipline are relaxed. Death leads to the physical dissolution of the body, of course, but from a pantheistic perspective an individual's death is part of the larger circle of life. For example, Faust descends to the mysterious realm of "the Mothers" in the second half of Goethe's drama, a place of "formation, transformation" (*Gestaltung, Umgestaltung*) into which old life dies, but out of which new life is born. Hans Castorp's journey up into the Alps is thus also a metaphorical descent to the underworld. Mann's most direct source is Wagner's *Tannhäuser*, in which the hero is seduced away from his sense of purpose in the world by Venus in her enchanted mountain, the "Hörselberg." The actual word *Zauberberg* (magic mountain) comes from *The Marble Image* (*Das Marmorbild*, 1817), a novella by the German romantic Joseph von Eichendorff about a man torn between his love for a chaste young woman and his desire for the seductive goddess Venus, but there are echoes of other mythical descents in works by Homer, Virgil, Dante, and Goethe in *The Magic Mountain*.

Castorp's journey is also a step out of time into timelessness. To be sure, time is precisely measured on the mountain, from the rigidly scheduled mealtimes and periods of rest to the patients' constant taking of their temperature and feeling their pulse. The very rhythm of the routine has a numbing effect on the patients, however, and the sense of movement through time is soon replaced with the impression that they are caught in an endlessly revolving cycle. Doctor Behrens, whom the patients dub Rhadamanthys, the mythical judge of the underworld, condemns his wards to ever-longer sentences that seem to stretch into eternity. Even the seasons do not follow their normal sequence on the mountain, as sun or snow can be expected at any time of year.

One of the most innovative aspects of *The Magic Mountain* is the way in which the subjective experience of time is mirrored in the structure of the novel. When Castorp arrives on the mountain, he has the sense that time has slowed down, because the day is packed with so many new experiences that it seems to go on forever – and each of these experiences is narrated in meticulous detail. As he gets used to the routine, however, days, weeks, and years begin to slip by with alarming rapidity – except that Castorp is not at all alarmed, for he drifts without resistance into the timeless world of a dream. And we drift with him, as each of the seven chapters becomes longer and narrates a longer stretch of time, until we, too, are rudely awakened at the end of the seventh chapter and the end of Castorp's seventh year by the sudden intrusion of the war.

While Mann structures his seemingly realistic narrative on the basis of ancient archetypes and myths, he also anchors the work in his contemporary reality by mapping it onto a symbolic landscape. The primary axis of the novel's symbolic geography is east–west: Germany is the "land of the center" between Eastern mysticism and Western rationalism. Mann's specific source for the allegedly Asiatic qualities of the Russians was Arthur Moeller van den Bruck's introduction to a German translation of Dostoevsky's complete works, but his description of the Slavic tendency toward passivity, formlessness, and irrationality also coincides with widespread Orientalist stereotypes. To the west lay France as a bastion of the Enlightenment and Italy as the home of the Renaissance (placing Italy to the west of Germany requires a stretch of the geographic imagination, but Mann's geographical symbolism works in broad stereotypes of national characters rather than in precise measurements of longitude and latitude). Further to the west lies Spain, which Mann describes as Russia's reverse mirror image or dialectical opposite in its overly rigid form and mystically tinged inclination toward violence.

Complicating the symbolic opposition between east and west is one between north and south, or, more specifically, between Europe and its colonies, which are linked to exoticism, sexuality, and violence. Mynheer Peeperkorn arrives from Java with his Malayan servant and commits suicide with cobra venom; a minor character named Herr Albin threatens to kill himself with a knife that he bought in Calcutta; an Egyptian lesbian gives Doctor Behrens a coffee service decorated with lewd pictures; the patients watch silent films with images of Japanese geishas, Balinese cockfights, wild elephants, and Oriental despots.

Unlike the members of the Buddenbrook family, Hans Castorp comes from Hamburg, not Lübeck; that is, from the city that made the leap from one of many medieval ports of the Hanseatic League to become the largest harbor in modern imperial Germany. Castorp's choice of reading matter, a book in English titled *Ocean Steamships*, and his chosen profession as a ship's engineer place him at the cutting edge of Germany's thrust toward economic and military might in competition with the British Empire. Other details suggest, however, that he is at heart a kindred spirit of the increasingly decadent Buddenbrooks after all: the death of his mother, father, and grandfather at an early age seems to sap his energy for life. Although he prepares for a career in modern industry, he is also fascinated by his grandfather's medieval-looking ceremonial garb and the baptismal font that symbolizes ancient tradition rather than modern progress. He also has a tendency to daydream, latent artistic talents, and a pleasurable addiction to the soporific effects of beer and tobacco. His stay at the sanatorium not only triggers the onset of a disease (although it is never entirely clear if Hans Castorp actually has an early stage of tuberculosis or if he simply catches a bad cold), but also strips aside the veneer of modern civilization and allows him to drift back into the dreams of his childhood.

Castorp's love for Clavdia Chauchat distracts him from his planned career on the Hamburg dockyards and ties him to the magic mountain. Romantic adventures are a standard feature of the *Bildungsroman*, or most novels, for that matter (as the etymological link between the French and German word for novel – *Roman* – and *romance* suggests). Mann's account of Castorp's shy flirtation with Chauchat, his awkward attempts at gallantry in the dining room, his ludicrous leering at Doctor Behrens' portrait of her in deep décolleté, and his rapturous babblings in French on the night that she finally permits him to sleep with her make for some of the most delightful passages in *The Magic Mountain*. On an allegorical level, Chauchat is a temptress who lures Castorp away from his duties and ensnares him in forbidden desires, like Eve or Venus or the Greek goddess Circe, who turns Odysseus' men into swine – just as Castorp borrows a pencil from Chauchat during the Mardi Gras party to draw a pig while blindfolded. In terms of the novel's symbolic geography, Chauchat combines Russian primitivism with French decadence. Chauchat is married to a Frenchman who is working in Daghestan, an oil-producing region in the Caucasus. She travels from one European sanatorium to the next, smokes, lives apart from her husband, and entertains other men behind closed doors – all symptoms of the modern, emancipated, western European woman. Yet her "Asiatic" features, exotic accent, and uncivilized tendency to arrive late, slam doors, and bite her fingernails remind us of her Russian origins and its symbolic ties to a pre-civilized "Oriental" world. Thus Chauchat, whose French name means "hot cat," represents a model of feminine sexuality that is both liberated from the constraints of civilized behavior and not yet subject to them.

But Clavdia Chauchat is also a man, or at least the reincarnation of a boy. The heterosexual romance is an example of the psychological phenomenon that Freud calls the return of the repressed, as Castorp only gradually realizes that Chauchat attracts him because she reminds him of Pribislav Hippe, a fellow student whom Castorp had loved as a boy. As was often the case when depicting homoerotic encounters, Mann drew on personal experience: Hippe is modeled on Williram Timpe, the son of a teacher in whose house Mann lived in his final year of high school, after his father had died and his mother had moved to Munich. The exchange of the pencil in the schoolyard and the secret hoarding of the treasured pencil shavings are based on fact: Mann recalls the incident in a diary entry of September 15, 1950. When he returned to Lübeck for the last time in May 1955 he visited his old school and again noted in his diary that he remembered "Willri Timpe, the second in the gallery" – that is, the gallery of boys or young men with whom he had been in love; the first was Armin Martens, already used for *Tonio Kröger*.

The relationship between Castorp's love for Clavdia Chauchat and his memories of Pribislav Hippe can be understood in at least three different ways. One could argue that Castorp undergoes what Freud would view as the normal progression from the confused sexual desires of childhood toward the successful resolution of the Oedipus complex, from adolescent homoeroticism to adult heterosexuality. The affair with Chauchat reminds him of a youthful phase that he has now left behind. One could also contend just the opposite: that the interest in Chauchat is merely a disguise for his fundamental homosexuality; desire for a slender-hipped woman who reminds him of a boy is the only socially acceptable way that Castorp can act on his homosexual fantasies. A third possibility is to leave the matter unresolved, in keeping with what Freud and Otto Weininger described as the essential bisexuality of human beings. Castorp desires both Hippe and Chauchat, male and female. While the nature of Castorp's desires may be ambiguous, his rejection of a certain type of aggressive masculinity is clear. When Chauchat returns to the sanatorium accompanied by Mynheer Peeperkorn, Castorp refuses to challenge his rival and insists instead that he believes in a gentler sort of masculinity in which distinctions between the genders become softened and blurred, an opinion that Mann echoed in his 1925 essay on "Marriage in Transition."

From Ludovico Settembrini's perspective, Clavdia Chauchat is nothing but a temptress that Castorp must avoid. Settembrini represents the humanism of the Italian Renaissance, the spirit of the Enlightenment, the French Revolution, and liberal nationalism. He is thus an embodiment of "civilization's literary man" whom Mann had attacked so ferociously in the *Reflections*, but now transformed into a largely sympathetic figure, in keeping with Mann's evolving political opinions. Settembrini is threadbare and chronically ill, but tirelessly dedicated to the cause of human freedom and full of fondness for Hans Castorp and concern for his well-being. He retreats on the evening of the

Mardi Gras party when he sees that he cannot stop Castorp's love for Chauchat, but Settembrini returns to do ideological battle with Leo Naphta in the second half of the novel.

Leo Naphta is another character who has drawn fire from those who suspect Mann of harboring anti-Semitic sentiments. Born the son of an eastern European kosher butcher who is brutally murdered in a pogrom, Naphta is raised by Jesuits, the militant wing of the Counter-Reformation. He is described as both physically ugly and intellectually dangerous, as he opposes Settembrini's enlightened humanism at every opportunity. Where Settembrini sees progress in the name of lofty ideals, Naphta sees monks toiling grimly in the effort to suppress their sexual desires; Settembrini contributes articles to an encyclopedia modeled on the project of the French Enlightenment, whereas Naphta treasures a grotesquely distorted Gothic Pieta; Settembrini is a freemason, as were many of the liberals who paved the way for the American and French Revolutions; Naphta argues that the seemingly enlightened organization has its roots in the sexually charged mysticism of ancient rituals and envisions a society of men held together in rigid discipline under the dictatorial control of an absolute leader.

Naphta's purpose in the novel is twofold. On the one hand, he serves as a monitory figure, a negative example and warning to those who would reject the Enlightenment and democracy. Settembrini may have his foibles, but Naphta is simply evil, or, to translate the opposition into Mann's contemporary political situation, the Weimar Republic may have its flaws, but the fascist alternative is unthinkable. On the other hand, Naphta complicates matters by turning Settembrini's arguments inside out. His point of view is both diametrically opposed to that of Settembrini and its dialectical inversion. The result moves what would seem to be a straightforward conflict between good and evil into an ambiguous realm in which a clever advocate can always dismantle the positions of his opponent.

The dialectical interplay between Settembrini and Naphta reminds us how Mann inverted his own arguments or those of others to suit his purpose at a given moment: Hans Blüher sees male–male eroticism as the basis of an authoritarian state. Mann turns the same argument into a celebration of democracy based on homoerotic bonds between men in "The German Republic," yet introduces renewed political ambiguity to the male-only organizations discussed in *The Magic Mountain*. Settembrini introduces the freemasons as the enlightened counterpart to the reactionary Jesuits, only to have Naphta call this distinction into question. The ambiguity of *The Magic Mountain* underscores a fundamental difference between Mann's essayistic interventions into his contemporary politics and his artistic practice. Mann is deadly serious when he urges his fellow Germans to throw their support behind the fledgling Republic, but in *The Magic Mountain*, direct polemics yield to negative dialectics that are not resolved into a final unambiguous synthesis.

Mann's inclusion of extended intellectual debates in *The Magic Mountain* distinguishes this work from *Buddenbrooks* and *Royal Highness* and aligns it with other modern German novels such as Robert Musil's *Man without Qualities* (*Der Mann ohne Eigenschaften*, 1931) and Hermann Broch's *Sleepwalkers* (*Die Schlafwanderer*, 1931–32). In the midst of even the most abstract arguments, however, Mann reminds us of the individual characters who are presenting these ideas: Settembrini speaks "plastically," with the overly precise articulation of someone who likes to hear himself talk; Naphta's voice grates like chalk dragged across a blackboard. Hans Castorp stands between them, sometimes listening intently, sometimes parroting back one idea or the other to the delight or dismay of his mentors.

Just when the endless play of words is becoming insufferable, a new character emerges who silences the sickly intellectuals by dint of his commanding presence. Mynheer Peeperkorn can rarely complete a sentence or a thought, and yet he exudes a charismatic aura of ravaged majesty. Mann based Peeperkorn's appearance and mannerisms on Gerhardt Hauptmann, who was deeply offended, but Mann did his diplomatic best to assure the older writer that the similarities were merely superficial and that he intended no harm. Like the allegorical figure of "Life" in *The Path to the Cemetery*, Peeperkorn is a representative of a vital force that goes beyond logic or language, but one that is corrupted from within. His malaria and the cobra venom that kills him are reminders of the colonial world where he was once master, but now its victim, just as Christian Buddenbrook has been infected with indolence by his long stay in the tropics and Gustav von Aschenbach succumbs to Asian cholera. Peeperkorn is also another parodied Christ figure: he hosts a bacchanalian Last Supper and sacrifices himself for no particular purpose other than that he is a dissipated old man who makes way for the younger rival – and to no avail, for as soon as he is gone, Clavdia also leaves for good.

Particularly poignant is the death of Castorp's beloved cousin Joachim Ziemssen. While Castorp gives in all too easily to the touch of illness that keeps him on the mountain, the much more seriously ill Ziemssen resists tooth and claw, eventually "deserting" the duty of his medical regime to return to his regiment. As Doctor Behrens had predicted, the decision proves fatal, for Joachim is forced to return in the company of his mother to the sanatorium, where he soon dies. Ziemssen is liked and respected by patients and staff, and although he is capable of a nasty comment about Leo Naphta's typically Jewish "puniness," he is a largely positive figure whose affectionate bond with Hans Castorp serves as an affirmation of friendship and love against the endless bickering between Naphta and Settembrini. It is all the more shocking, then, that this good soldier should be the plaything of a séance conducted by the in-house psychologist Dr. Edhin Krokowski, another eastern European whose place of origin and choice of profession suggest that he might also be Jewish. Thomas Mann was interested in magic and the occult. He attended several séances in Munich in the early 1920s and wrote an essay on his "Occult Experiences" ("Okkulte Erlebnisse," 1924) that was a hit on the lecture circuit. In the context of *The Magic Mountain*, however, the séance that successfully summons Joachim Ziemssen back from the dead is rejected by Hans Castorp as a distasteful affair that violates his cousin's dignity.

The meaning of *The Magic Mountain* comes down to the tension established between Hans Castorp's vision in the snow and our final glimpse of him on the battlefields of the First World War. Against doctor's orders, Castorp goes off skiing on his own and gets lost in a blinding snowstorm. He has a vision that amounts to an allegorical depiction of Nietzsche's *Birth of Tragedy*, as he sees images of Dionysian horror and Apollinian beauty, horrible hags devouring a human sacrifice and handsome young men and women strolling in the sunshine. The vision sparks a flash of insight that is italicized in the text: "*For the sake of goodness and love, man should not allow death to rule his thoughts.*" In other words, one should be aware of the dark forces at work in the human psyche, but one should choose the light of reason in the end. Mann would make just this argument with increasing urgency in his essays of the coming years, but in the context of the novel, the binding force of the insight is undermined by the immediate context and the novel's conclusion. Castorp is sick, dizzy from the high altitude, and has had a shot of brandy before he has his vision; by the time that he staggers back to the sanatorium, he has already begun to forget what he has learned. When we see him for the last time, he is singing a romantic song about death as he runs across a muddy battlefield with little hope that he will survive. In the place of a clear-cut polemic in favor of "life," Mann has left us with the memory of the affection between Hans Castorp and his cousin, and the hope that someday, when the carnage of war has passed, that love will rise again.

Chapter 5

The struggle against National Socialism

Thomas Mann's fame rose to new heights in the years between the publication of *The Magic Mountain* in late 1924 and Hitler's seizure of power on January 30, 1933. Mann lectured frequently in Germany and throughout Europe, was a prominent member of the PEN Club, and was awarded the Nobel Prize for Literature. The times were nevertheless trying for Mann, as the political movement that he had dismissed as nonsense in 1921 was proving very serious indeed. As the power of the National Socialists grew, Mann became increasingly vocal in his opposition to them. At times Mann intervened directly in political discussions, most famously in his 1930 "Address to the Germans: An Appeal to Reason" ("Deutsche Ansprache: Ein Appell an die Vernunft"). Mann spoke on October 17, 1930 in the same hall in Berlin in which he had delivered "The German Republic" in 1922; then he had spoken in the wake of Rathenau's assassination, now he spoke in the immediate aftermath of the National Socialists' first major victory at the polls.

Mann begins by noting that he was supposed to read from his new novel, but that such a reading would be inappropriate under the circumstances. Instead, he urges the Germans in the strongest possible language to turn away from fanaticism, from a "dictatorship of violence," from "politics as the mass opiate of the Third Reich," and to work instead for greater human dignity, rationality, and a responsible Social Democracy. Goebbels had gotten wind of Mann's intentions shortly before the event and sent twenty SA men in rented tuxedos to disrupt the lecture. Mann spoke over a mixture of heckling and applause and then managed to exit the hall through a little-known passageway with the help of the conductor Bruno Walter, who had performed frequently in the building and was familiar with its nooks and crannies.

Direct confrontation followed by a dramatic escape was not typical for Mann. More frequently he addressed the political situation obliquely in his essays. In seeking to understand the appeal of the Nazis, Mann did not look to economic explanations such as the traumatic effect of the uncontrolled inflation of 1923 or the collapse of the stock market in 1929. He focused instead on the low self-esteem of the little man and the irresponsible infatuation on the part of intellectuals with philosophical irrationalism. "I know that I am nothing" was the way Mann described the mentality of the masses that supported Hitler, "but at least I am not a Jew."[1] Worse were those intellectuals who should have known better and spoken out against the rising tide of German National Socialism, but instead embraced philosophies that leant tacit or direct support to the fascist cause. In 1926, for instance, Mann traveled to Paris where he was feted by some of the liberal French intellectuals he had opposed so bitterly during the First World War. In his extensive autobiographical account of this visit, Mann criticized a new edition of Johann Jakob Bachofen's works that had been published with a lengthy introduction by Alfred Baeumler, a future Nazi ideologue, because he felt that it advocated a "revolutionary obscurantism" that was better avoided under present circumstances.[2] In 1929, Mann praised Lessing as a representative of the Enlightenment and described Freud as a modern-day heir to Novalis, in that both were romantics who understood the power of dreams and desires and yet looked to the ultimate triumph of reason over irrationalism, light over darkness. In 1932, Mann celebrated Goethe as an open-minded German cosmopolitan, as opposed to militant, narrow-minded nationalists;[3] in the same year, he also revised his earlier essay on Goethe and Tolstoy to stress Germany's need to abandon its *Sonderweg* (separate path) and to establish closer ties with the West.

Given Mann's consistent opposition to the National Socialists and their ideological apologists, one might have expected him to be one of the first to speak out publicly against Hitler when he was named chancellor, but this was not the case. Mann also did not actively go into exile; he happened to be out of the country on a lecture tour and was warned by his children not to return to Munich. The distinction would be trivial except for the fact that it marks the beginning of a four-year period in which Mann hesitated to come out publicly against the Nazi regime. We can follow Mann's moods closely, for he began a new diary in exile that continues with minor interruptions until a few days before his death. From the beginning, Mann was unequivocal in his private rejection of a regime that he labeled "bestial," "disgusting," and "idiotic." He was uncertain, however, whether or not he should speak out in public. When Heinrich and Klaus Mann began a journal, *The Collection* (*Die Sammlung*, 1933), Mann initially agreed to contribute but withdrew from the project when it turned out to be more politically outspoken than he had anticipated. On more than one occasion, Mann began writing a political essay, only to put it back in the drawer and turn to something innocuous, like his long description of how he read *Don Quixote* while on his first ocean voyage to America.

In January 1936, Mann was finally goaded to take a public stand. The exiled Leopold Schwarzschild accused Mann's publisher Gottfried Bermann-Fischer of having accommodated himself to the Nazis while he remained in Germany. According to Schwarzschild, all German writers worthy of the name were now in exile. Eduard Korrodi, a Swiss journalist, weighed into the debate on January 26, 1936, pointing out that many prominent German authors had in fact remained in Germany or at least, like Mann, had continued to publish their works in Germany. The emigrant community consisted only of a few, primarily Jewish, authors. Until this time, Mann had kept his distance from the other émigrés, but now he was forced to make a decision: either he could ignore Korrodi's article and thus implicitly endorse its argument, or he could contest its claims and declare his solidarity with the exile community. Under strong pressure from Erika and Klaus, Mann chose the latter. On February 3, 1936, he sent an open letter to Korrodi in which he pointed out that many of those in exile, including Heinrich and himself, were not Jewish. He went on to condemn the Nazi hatred of the Jews as symptomatic of a deadly sort of xenophobic nationalism that would isolate Germany from the rest of Europe and its own cosmopolitan tradition. "Nothing good can come from the current German rulers," Mann concluded, "not for Germany, and not for the world."

Mann knew that he had burned his bridges with Nazi Germany at this point, but as he explained in a letter of February 9, 1936 to Hermann Hesse, "I had to show my colors." It took some time before the government reacted, perhaps because they wanted to preserve appearances during the Berlin Olympics in the summer of 1936, but in November Mann learned that his German citizenship was to be revoked and that the University of Bonn was planning to take back his honorary doctorate. With little more to lose at this point (Mann had secretly procured Czech citizenship in November 1936), Mann wrote an open letter to the dean of the university in which he stated that he could no longer remain silent. Politics and art had become hopelessly entwined in Germany's totalitarian state, and that state had brought nothing but horror and ruin to Germany; now it was on the brink of starting a war that would threaten the entire world. Stop now, he concluded, while there is still time to reverse course and rejoin the European community. "God help our darkened and abused land and teach it to make peace with the world and with itself!"

The letter was published on January 20, 1937 in Switzerland and was soon reprinted in Germany, translated, and distributed throughout the world; by

March 20,000 copies in German alone had been printed. Because of its wide circulation, uncompromising language, and the high profile of its author, some have claimed that it was the single most important public statement by a German against the National Socialist regime. But why did Mann hesitate for so long to speak out? Mann's enemies rumored that he was secretly sympathetic with the regime, but the diaries provide ample proof that Mann had nothing but contempt for the Nazis. If he had wanted to return, he would have been welcomed by a government seeking the appearance of legitimacy. Whether they would have been willing to look the other way at Katia's Jewish origins is another question. Like many assimilated Jews, Katia's parents refused to believe that they would be victimized by the Nazis and managed to escape to Switzerland only at the very last minute. The far more outspoken Heinrich was already on the Nazi hit-list, as were Erika and Klaus – as a political dissident, the son of an assimilated Jew, and an open homosexual, Klaus Mann was a walking catalog of everything the Nazis disdained.

Mann's diaries do contain a few damning asides in which he states that under different circumstances he would not entirely disagree with the Nazis' treatment of the Jews. These statements must be balanced against others in which he expresses outrage and disgust at the persecution of the Jews, and, as we have seen, Mann signaled his solidarity with the Jewish émigrés in his open letter to Eduard Korrodi. In the early 1920s, Mann was still able to deny the extent of German prejudice, but the Nazis forced him to confront a level of state-sponsored anti-Semitism that went far beyond anything he could have imagined and that provoked his public outrage and private horror. Even now, however, Mann continued to harbor ambivalent feelings about the Jews in general and to make occasionally nasty asides about individual Jews who got on his nerves – his in-laws, for instance.

There were other factors that contributed to Mann's reluctance to speak out against the Nazis. Without the benefit of hindsight, it was not immediately clear how long the regime would last or how bad it would get. Or at least Mann sometimes tried to convince himself that this was the case. As late as January 20, 1933, Mann had insisted in a letter to Walter Opitz that things were not quite as bad as they seemed, recalling his notorious contention in 1921 that the Germans would never be openly anti-Semitic! "Human capacity for self-deception is astounding," as Mann's narrator will comment wryly in *Joseph and his Brothers* (p. 828). Financial concerns were real and pressing: soon after it became clear that Mann was not planning to return to Germany, the Nazis confiscated his villa and his automobiles and froze his bank accounts. One of the reasons that Mann avoided a public break with the regime was that he was hoping to get back his money and possessions. Mann was also on the verge of publishing his first major work since *The Magic Mountain* and he wanted to make sure that the first three volumes of his Joseph tetralogy appeared in Germany, which they did: *The Stories of Jacob* came out in October 1933, followed by *Young Joseph* in March 1934 and *Joseph in Egypt* in 1936; only *Joseph the Provider* would be published much later in exile. Mann's publications were his primary source of income, after all, and he did not want to lose touch with the nation that he felt he represented.

Once Mann made his public break with the Nazi regime, he became committed as few others in the German exile community to its defeat. Again and again, Mann urged the Germans to abjure their allegiance to fascism and to commit themselves to the principles of the Enlightenment and the politics of Western democracy. In New York, Mann spoke at mass rallies in Madison Square Garden and Carnegie Hall. He crisscrossed the continent from Los Angeles to Toronto and from Seattle to San Antonio, speaking out against Hitler's Germany. Beginning in 1940, Mann delivered a series of radio addresses to the German people that the BBC broadcast into Germany in an effort to counter the propaganda of the totalitarian state. Recordings of the broadcasts have been preserved, and one can still listen to Mann's somewhat high-pitched, impassioned delivery of the short speeches. Although he was still deeply committed to his ongoing literary projects, Mann regularly interrupted his work to write these and other political essays. Mann condemned the British policy of appeasement, chafed at the American reluctance to enter into the war, and accepted with equanimity the Allied destruction of German cities, including his hometown of Lübeck. As he reminded his German listeners, they had sowed the wind by bombing Coventry; now they were reaping the whirlwind.

Despite the scattered private comments about certain annoying Jewish individuals, Mann repeatedly declared his public allegiance to the Jews and condemned their persecution by the Nazis. Mann denounced the state-sponsored pogrom of November 9, 1938 ("Kristallnacht"), broadcast news into Germany about hundreds of Dutch Jews who had been used for horrible medical experiments before being executed ("They were just Jews, after all" – *es waren ja Juden*),[4] and registered his shame and revulsion when the concentration camps were revealed to the world in early 1945. If he still claimed that the Jews were different, it was to insist that that difference be preserved to enrich Germany and Europe, not eradicated in the name of ethnic cleansing or racial purity. One of Mann's repeated refrains in his political essays of the 1930s and 1940s is that nationalism based on internal homogeneity and external aggression is wrong; rather than trying to make Europe German, the Germans should become more European; they should be tolerant cosmopolitans, not bigoted nationalists and militant imperialists.

A final characteristic of Mann's wartime journalism is his rejection of the notion that there is a "good Germany" and a "bad Germany" – here Beethoven, there Hitler; here Goethe, there Goebbels. As Mann viewed it, the conflicting forces were always intertwined, particularly in such powerful figures as Luther, Wagner, and Nietzsche. Mann's effort was directed against the sort of easy excuses that would become notorious after the war: "It was all Hitler's fault; I had nothing to do with it." "I was just following orders." From Mann's perspective, coming to terms with Nazi Germany could not take the form of self-righteous finger-pointing at the evil in others, but rather in the struggle against the evil within oneself. Thus, in 1938, Mann wrote an essay about Hitler not as an alien being, but as an embarrassing relative ("Bruder Hitler," translated as "That Man is My Brother"), and he repeated the same argument in a major essay on "Germany and the Germans" marking the end of the war: "there are not two Germanies, one good and one evil, but only one; the evil Germany is the good one that went astray. I have it all within me, too; I have experienced it myself."

Joseph and his Brothers

Mann's major literary project between the years 1925 and 1943 was *Joseph and his Brothers*, a work that expanded the familiar biblical story in the last fifteen chapters of Genesis into a four-volume novel of some two thousand pages. The initial impetus came in 1925, when Mann was asked to write a brief introduction to a volume of illustrations on the theme of Joseph in Egypt. The invitation reawakened fond memories of a book about ancient Egypt that Mann had enjoyed as a child and also reminded him of a passage in Goethe's autobiography in which he remarked that someone really ought to flesh out the terse biblical narrative into a full-length novel.

The sheer size of *Joseph and his Brothers*, the deliberate pace of the narration, and the inclusion of many arcane details about ancient Egyptian theology may discourage many readers from devoting the time and energy to discover this richly rewarding work of modern fiction. Although it starts slowly and the early episodes are narrated out of sequence, the outlines of the familiar story eventually emerge: Joseph is sold into slavery by his jealous brothers and taken to Egypt, where he becomes Potiphar's most trusted slave. He is thrown into prison when falsely accused of trying to seduce Potiphar's wife, only to be released when he is able to interpret Pharaoh's dreams. He prepares Egypt for the coming famine and is ultimately reunited with his brothers and his father, Jacob. Patience is required, however, for Mann fleshes out the skeletal plot with subtle psychological portraits of the characters involved and minutely detailed recreations of the conversations they might have had, while embedding it all in a dense network of mythical allusions and philosophical speculations. Mann's expansion of his brief biblical source to enormous proportions is in keeping with the conviction expressed in the preface to *The Magic Mountain* that a story must be told in detail if it is to be truly entertaining. As Mann had stated already in the essay "Bilse and I" ("Bilse und ich," 1906), what matters in his fiction is not what happens, but how those events are described; not the originality of plot, but the breathing of new life into old stories. A second function of the minute detail is to give the sense of an ancient Egyptian court society based on ritual and etiquette, where circumlocution is the norm and ceremony replaces substance. Potiphar is awarded the lofty title of Pharaoh's "sole and true friend," although he is not really Pharaoh's friend at all; Potiphar makes a great show of his virility on dangerous hippopotamus hunts, but is actually an overweight eunuch. By linking the Old Testament story to a larger Judeo-Christian tradition, as well as to ancient Greek, Babylonian, and Egyptian mythology, finally, Mann seeks to transform a sacred text of the Jewish tradition into a work about humanity as a whole.

Mann's primary source was Luther's translation of Genesis, together with biblical commentaries and books about ancient Egypt. Of the latter, Arthur Weigall's *The Life and Times of Akhnaton* (1910; translated to German 1923) was particularly important, as it gives a detailed account of the Egyptian pharaoh who broke with centuries of religious tradition in the effort to impose a strictly monotheistic religion on his people. Howard Carter made his sensational discovery of King Tutankhamun's tomb in 1922, which sparked a craze for ancient Egypt throughout Europe for the rest of the decade; Mann notes in his account of his visit to Paris in 1926 that he discussed the discoveries with Egyptologists there. In the previous year, in fact, a German steamship line had given Thomas Mann a free Mediterranean cruise, complete with a whirlwind tour of the major attractions in Egypt, in return for an account of the journey that Mann wrote for a popular journal. He made a second visit to Egypt in 1930, giving him the opportunity to witness first-hand the land that he had previously known only through books. The most important biblical commentary that Mann used was Alfred Jeremias' *Das alte Testament*, a leading work of the "Pan-Babylonian School" of biblical interpretation. Jeremias argued that the stories of Genesis were not peculiar to the ancient Hebrews, but that they emerged out of an earlier Babylonian tradition and had much in common with other ancient religions of the Mediterranean region.

"Deep is the well of the past" (*Tief ist der Brunnen der Vergangenheit*) (p. 3). Mann begins the prelude to his four-volume novel with this brief, if somewhat enigmatic, sentence. His narrator goes on to explain that looking for the origins of human civilization is like looking into an almost bottomless well. There must have been a moment of creation, just as there was surely a first time for everything that has happened since, but the events that have been recorded as the first were almost certainly already repetitions of previous events: the flood described in Genesis was surely not *the* flood, but a later calamity that was subsequently confused with the first. "The well of the past" or the "underworld" that he describes here are other terms for the timeless presence that he associates elsewhere with Nietzsche's Dionysian realm, Schopenhauer's will, or the concept of the medieval *nunc stans* that Hans Castorp discovers on the magic mountain. To put it another way, *Joseph and his Brothers* begins where Hans Castorp ends up before the outbreak of the war: suspended in a moment where time seems to stand still. As Mann's narrator explains, the idea that there is a well of timeless presence beneath the sequence of individual moments is an esoteric truth grasped only by a few initiates. This insight is rendered accessible to the masses through rituals and myths. Each year leaves fall, winter comes, and nature dies, only to be born again each spring; the various Mediterranean religions reenact the cycles of nature in symbolic form through myths and rituals about the death and resurrection of a god, whether he is the Babylonian Tammuz, the Greek Adonis, or the Egyptian Osiris. There is movement within the cycle, but no progress, for the cycle simply repeats itself over and over again.

Mann structures the plot of *Joseph and his Brothers* on this pattern of ritual death and symbolic rebirth: after tricking his twin brother Esau out of Isaac's blessing, Jacob must flee to the "underworld" of his uncle Laban, who forces his homeless nephew to work seven years to win Rachel as his bride – and seven more years after he tricks him into marrying Leah first. Joseph suffers three descents to the underworld: his brothers cast him into the well and then sell him into slavery; he is sold again to Potiphar by Midianite traders; and he is cast into prison after Potiphar's wife accuses him of attempted rape. But Joseph's repeated "resurrections" are not merely repetitions but also signs of progress, as he rises from Potiphar's slave to become Akhnaton's right-hand man. On an individual level, *Joseph and his Brothers* is another *Bildungsroman*, the story of the hero's maturation from a naïve youth to a mature leader who is at once visionary, just, and politically shrewd. Joseph's individual development is also part of a larger transformation of mythic repetition into Judeo-Christian salvation history. Jacob's primary concern is to pass on his special blessing to future generations; his lineage will eventually lead through David to Jesus Christ, who is referred to in *Joseph and his Brothers* as Shiloh, the promised one. Unlike the eternally recurring cycles of ancient myth, Christian salvation history knows progress as well as repetition: Christ's resurrection is both a reenactment of Jonah's emergence from the belly of the whale and the fulfillment of a promise on the road to salvation.

Mann's purpose in *Joseph and his Brothers* is not to give a lesson in Judeo-Christian theology, however, but to tell the story of human progress from polytheism to monotheism, superstition to reason, brute force to planned government, and from the collective to the individual. His method is syncretic, blending together multiple ancient myths and modern philosophies – thus Joseph "is" Tammuz, Osiris, Adonis, and Christ. His personal maturation stands for the story of human progress that Bachofen describes in terms of the movement from the "hetaerism" of undisciplined human sexuality in primitive societies through matriarchy to patriarchy, or what Freud depicts as the successful resolution of the Oedipus conflict on the individual level and the internalization of the paternal super-ego for society as a whole. On yet another level, *Joseph and his Brothers* retells the story of Wagner's Ring cycle, beginning with the preface that ripples up from the depths of time and concluding with the twilight of the gods and the dawn of humanity. Mann's "message" is the same as the one he formulates in the italicized line in the "Snow" chapter of *The Magic Mountain* and in the essays that he wrote when he periodically interrupted his work on *Joseph and his Brothers*: we must be aware of the underworld, of the fathomless depths of the well, but we must nevertheless climb toward the light. Conceived in the spirit of Mann's new-found commitment to humanism and the Weimar Republic in the mid-1920s, *Joseph and his Brothers* grew into the fictional counterpart of his non-fictional interventions into politics over the next two decades. In it, as he repeatedly claimed, Mann sought to wrest myth from the hands of the fascists and place it once again in the service of human progress and enlightenment.

Joseph and his Brothers is far more than a heartfelt plea for the values of civilization in the face of cultural barbarism, however, for it is also a self-contained fictional world with fully realized characters and a political and symbolic landscape of its own. When looking back at his first novel, Mann once said that he had initially planned to write only about Hanno Buddenbrook, but soon realized that to tell the story properly, he had to begin with earlier generations. The same is true of his treatment of Joseph's story, which goes all the way back to the Creation and devotes an entire volume to *The Stories of Jacob*. Joseph's father emerges as a fascinating character as Mann conceives him: he is distinguished by his fierce commitment to monotheism and an inclination to ponder religious mysteries that sometimes distract him from practical affairs. Jacob is fascinated to the point of obsession with the notion of mythic repetition, the idea that his life follows the patterns of previous generations. As a result, his sense of individual identity is relatively weak; as the narrator puts it, it is difficult to talk about people who do not know who they are. In accordance with the feeling that his personal history merges with those of his ancestors, the stories of his life are not told in chronological order. Thus *The Stories of Jacob* begins with a conversation between Jacob and his seventeen-year-old son Joseph at the well, jumps back to an encounter between Jacob and his nephew Eliphaz that took place long before Joseph was born, moves forward to a much later encounter with Esau, only to jump back again to the famous story in which Jacob tricks his father Isaac into blessing him rather than his brother. Interspersed with these episodes are repeated references to other individuals and events from the book of Genesis. Only when Jacob is in exile in the land of Laban does the narrative settle down into a straightforward chronological flow.

Jacob has a sense of dignity about him that impresses those he encounters; even his hostile uncle Laban quickly realizes that Jacob is a man of blessing. Yet he has character flaws as well: his inclination toward religious pondering can also serve as a convenient way to avoid unpleasant reality, as in the case when his sons butcher the inhabitants of a town where a prominent citizen has eloped with their sister Dinah. He is capable of hard work and deep love for Rachel, Joseph, and Benjamin, but he can also be duplicitous, vindictive, and a bit of a charlatan. For these reasons, some have argued that Jacob is yet another character in Mann's fiction that embodies certain negative Jewish stereotypes, although in comparison with a figure such as Naphta, Jacob is on balance far more sympathetically portrayed. His sons, however, exhibit a repeated tendency toward what Mann termed *Rückfälligkeit*, literally the tendency to "fall back" into pre-civilized patterns of behavior, not only in their excessive punishment of Dinah's fiancé and his townspeople, but also in their brutal beating of Joseph and their willingness to sell him into slavery. In a short essay, "Against Stupidity and Retrograde Behavior" ("Gegen Dickfelligkeit und Rückfälligkeit," 1927), Mann drew direct parallels between these episodes in his fiction and the growing threat of anti-civilized barbarism in his contemporary political reality.

Against such behavior, Joseph stands out for his ability to learn from his mistakes, his compassion for his father's suffering, and his willingness to forgive his brothers. *Young Joseph* tells of the gifted and beautiful but also spoiled and naïve child who inadvertently provokes his brothers' rage. *Joseph in Egypt* depicts a young man who is careful not to antagonize his potential enemies as he rises to a position of authority in Potiphar's house. The chief threat to his position and the cause of his eventual downfall is the potential seduction by Potiphar's wife. In contrast to the brief biblical account, Mann gives Potiphar's wife a name (Mut-em-enet or simply Mut), a psychological profile, and a political context. Mut is the virgin wife of the eunuch Potiphar, who was castrated by his parents – who are also twin brother and sister – in a misguided effort to elevate him above base physical desire. Until she begins to notice Joseph, Mut has never been troubled by sexual desires and only gradually realizes the extent to which she is in love. Mann's depiction of Mut is a masterful study of self-deception, sexual obsession, and debasement, as a woman of the highest Egyptian nobility gradually yields to an overwhelming passion for a foreign slave. Mann's character study unfortunately also has elements of misogyny and racism: the more threatening Mut becomes in her forbidden passion for Joseph, the more female she seems, as her breasts swell and she becomes consumed with lust.

Mut-em-enet is a grandiose example of the sort of femmes fatales that have haunted Mann's fiction from the beginning. At the height of her passion, Mut also employs the services of a slave named Tabubu, who has black skin, leathery breasts, and is practiced in the wicked magic of Negro lands. Together they cast magic spells and perform mystic rites, including animal sacrifice under a full moon. Although Mut eventually embodies female sexuality at its most threatening, the narrator is at pains to defend her against the charge that she is nothing but a calculating seductress from the beginning and a vindictive jilted lover at the end, stressing instead the amount of time involved in her attraction to Joseph and power of the desires that enslave her. The evil court dwarf Dudu initially encourages Mut's interest in Joseph in the conviction that this is the surest way to bring about Joseph's downfall, and he nearly succeeds. In the end, however, it is Mut-em-enet who is undone by sexual desires that shatter her carefully constructed public persona.

Mut-em-enet's personal downfall plays out against a religio-political background – and as the narrator reminds us, there was no difference in ancient Egypt between the religious and the political. From Jacob's perspective, all of Egypt is a realm of obscenity, superstition, and blackness – in short, Egypt is the underworld. The actual political landscape that Mann traces in *Joseph and his Brothers* is more complex, however. The Hebrews are a nomadic people who followed Abraham out of Babylon and wandered as far as Egypt before settling in the area of Palestine. In the course of their travels, they have adopted foreign fashions, learned foreign languages, and married into other peoples. Their sense of being a "chosen people" lies therefore not in any sense of cultural or racial purity, but rather in their strict monotheism and the conviction that a blessing can be passed down from one generation to the next. They live on the outskirts of the Egyptian Empire, which is portrayed as an ancient civilization in a late phase of its history. The Egyptians find it difficult to maintain control over colonies conquered by previous generations, and their capital city, Thebes, has become the multi-cultural hub of a sprawling empire, full of people of every race and shape from their colonies and the rest of the known world.

The Egyptians oscillate between disdain for everything foreign and an attraction to the exotic. The ambivalence carries over into their two major religions. The followers of Amun-Re adhere to a xenophobic nationalism that bears a transparent similarity to Nazi ideology, while Akhnaton and his court believe in Atum-Re, a universal monotheistic God who is tolerant and cosmopolitan. As a Hebrew in Egypt, Joseph is both the target of prejudice on the part of some and the object of fascination on the part of others; he is clever enough to guard against persecution from the former and to profit from his appeal to the latter. Joseph's main rival for Potiphar's favor is Dudu, a follower of Amun-Re who bitterly resents the rise of the foreign slave. Also aligned with Amun-Re are Beknechons, a zealous priest, and Mut-em-enet, whereas the courtier Potiphar inclines toward Akhnaton's more open-minded Atum-Re. Mut's attraction to the foreign Joseph is therefore in conflict with her religious principles as well as being potentially adulterous and in violation of class distinctions. As a sign of her increasing infatuation with Joseph, Mut begins to dress in foreign clothing that reminds Joseph of his mother, Rachel. When he finally rejects her, however, Mut's distended breasts shrivel up and she becomes more bigoted than she was before.

Joseph the Provider depicts Joseph's rise from prison to become Akhnaton's second-in-command, his reconciliation with his brothers, and his reunion with his father. Mann portrays Akhnaton as a moody teenager given to migraines and theological speculation about his monotheistic religion. In his detachment from day-to-day affairs he resembles Jacob, although with potentially more serious political consequences: Jacob is the patriarch of a nomadic family, while Akhnaton is the leader of a vast but crumbling empire soon to be challenged by years of famine. Acting on the advice of his politically savvy mother, Akhnaton appoints Joseph to prepare for the coming calamity, and Joseph quickly takes command. He strengthens the internal unity of the Egyptian nation by revising the tax structure and cracking down on wealthy landowners who owe money to the government. He also stockpiles food to prepare for the coming famine, which has the indirect result of shoring up the crumbling Egyptian empire, as otherwise hostile powers and rebellious colonies are forced to pay dearly for scraps from the Egyptian table.

Joseph the Provider is the segment of *Joseph and his Brothers* most easily read as a political allegory: the fanatical nationalist Beknechons resembles Goebbels, the politically inept Akhnaton bears certain similarities to Neville

Chamberlain and his policy of appeasement, and Joseph in his role as the Egyptian provider reminds readers of Franklin Delano Roosevelt and his New Deal. Thomas Mann was outspoken in his admiration for the American president, whom he met on two occasions, both for the policies that helped to pull America out of the Depression and for his leadership in the Allied effort to defeat Hitler. In keeping with his patrician origins, Mann was not interested in Roosevelt as a champion of the little man, but rather in his role as a benevolent dictator, as a visionary leader who was willing to bend the rules, if necessary, in the effort to guide his people along the right path.

Disorder and Early Sorrow and *Mario and the Magician*

The roughly seventeen years that Mann needed to complete *Joseph and his Brothers* were not only a time of unprecedented turmoil in Mann's personal life and in world politics, but also a period of tremendous accomplishments. In addition to the massive biblical novel and a steady stream of essays on literary topics and political events, Mann maintained a voluminous correspondence and still found time for daily diary entries. During these same years, Mann also completed a number of smaller literary projects, including four novellas and a novel, *Lotte in Weimar*. While *Joseph and his Brothers* is his major work of the period – some would say the major work of his entire career – these shorter texts are more accessible to the general reader and more suited for classroom discussion.

After straining to complete a long novel, Mann sometimes relaxed by focusing his energies on a relatively short novella. Thus after *The Magic Mountain* was published in late 1924, Mann wrote *Disorder and Early Sorrow* (*Unordnung und frühes Leid*) in the spring of 1925; when he completed *Joseph and his Brothers* in January 1943, he dashed off *The Tables of the Law* (*Das Gesetz*) in February and March. Actually, Mann never "dashed off" anything; he continued to write slowly but steadily. The remarkable volume of the writing that he left behind – in the form of fiction, essays, letters, and diary entries – is a tribute to his longevity and what he termed *Beharrlichkeit* (perseverance), a word implying both discipline and determination.

Disorder and Early Sorrow marks a return to the openly autobiographical subject-matter of the idylls written shortly after the First World War, although this time Mann felt that he had gotten it right: in his "Lebensaufriss" (Outline of My Life, 1930) he declared that *Disorder and Early Sorrow* was superior to the *Song of the Little Child*; ten years later in "On Myself" he declared it one of his best. The minimal plot of the novella centers on the spoiled but precocious teenage children of a professor and his wife who throw a party for their friends. The "disorder" refers in the first instance to the faux-bohemian atmosphere among the privileged youth of the intellectual and artistic milieu – the narrator refers to them ironically as the "villa proletariat" (*Villenproletarier*).[5] The five-year-old little sister goes to bed sobbing because she has a crush on one of her older sibling's friends, hence the "early sorrow." Behind the older children "Ingrid" and "Bert" it is easy to identify Erika and Klaus; Little Eleanor or Lorchen is five in the story, matching her with Mann's youngest daughter, Elisabeth, and the youngest boy, referred to in the story only by a derogatory nickname, "Biter," has his real-life model in Michael, Mann's youngest son. The mother, who is worn down by her daily struggle to find food for her large family, corresponds closely to Katia in her role as the family provider during the difficult postwar years. The novella again reflects Mann's blatant prejudices regarding his children: the young daughter for whom he had written the *Song of the Little Child* remains irresistibly charming, while Michael's fictional counterpart is prone to wild tantrums and is not worthy of a real name. Yet the differences between the real Mann family and the figures depicted in *Disorder and Early Sorrow* are equally striking: Thomas Mann was not a tenured professor of history and there are no characters in the novella that correspond to his middle children, Golo and Monika. As always, there is as much imaginative deformation in the story as there is autobiographical revelation. The self-styled "seismograph" has once again transformed personal confession into an encapsulated image of the spirit of the age.

The autobiographical background allows us to date the events depicted in *Disorder and Early Sorrow* in 1923, the year of the great German inflation. Erika was born in 1905, Klaus in 1906, and Elisabeth in 1918; in the novella, Ingrid is eighteen, Bert seventeen, and Lorchen five. Under the weight of crippling war reparations, the German government was unable to pay its debts or balance its budget, so it simply printed more money – a lot more money. In January 1919, one dollar was worth 8.9 German Marks; three years later the exchange rate was nearly 200 Marks to the dollar. By January 1923, the rate was over 17,000 to 1, and by November of that same year it had soared to an astonishing four trillion to one. At that point, the government stepped in to stabilize the currency, but the economic and psychological damage was done: millions who had lived within their means and saved prudently for retirement found themselves destitute. Seeming fiscal virtue had been punished with abject poverty, creating a widespread sense of bewilderment and bitterness. Not coincidentally, Adolf Hitler staged his "Beer-Hall Putsch" on November 9, 1923, and although this first attempt to gain power failed, it marked the beginning of the rise to power of a party that capitalized on the confused desires of a people traumatized by military defeat and economic disaster.

Although in better financial shape than most Germans, Thomas Mann also suffered substantial losses to his inheritance and savings due to inflation. Looking back at the period twenty years later, Mann remembered the widespread suffering caused by the unchecked inflation and also recalled a tragicomic story about his own misfortune: during the war he had invested 10,000 Marks in the country estate of a friend. In the spring of 1923, the friend told Mann that he was forced to put the house on the market and that he was therefore returning Mann's money – in fact, the very same bills that Mann had given him in 1917, except that now they were utterly worthless. "There I stood, somewhat disbelieving, somewhat embarrassed, still not quite comprehending, with the clean, almost new, attractively printed museum pieces in my hand."[6]

Disorder and Early Sorrow also makes reference to the surreal world in which an egg cost 6,000 Marks and a glass of beer 8,000, but Mann's primary purpose is not to chronicle the changing exchange rate, but rather to depict a social order that is rapidly coming unraveled. Professor Cornelius is just barely able to retain the villa bought in more prosperous times, but the appearance of the shabbily clad family now clashes with what was once the suitably opulent frame for their upper-middle-class existence. Cornelius loves history, but only if it is safely in the past; now he is confronted with "unhistorical" times (p. 186), when everything is in flux and the outcome still uncertain. His response to historical change is ambivalent: Professor Cornelius is preparing for a seminar on the Spanish Counter-Reformation, which he describes as a valiant but hopeless struggle to hold back the tide of historical progress unleashed by German Protestantism. His position recalls Mann's own in his preface to the *Reflections of a Nonpolitical Man*, where he characterizes his essay as a rearguard defense of a lost cause. By 1925, however, Mann had reluctantly but emphatically endorsed the new Weimar Republic, thus signaling a willingness to adapt to changing times that distinguishes him from Professor Cornelius. In private life, Cornelius witnesses empathetically but also helplessly his daughter's infatuation with a young man, reminding him that here, too, change is inevitable and that his beloved child will eventually turn her affections away from him.

Lacking the memories and the financial concerns of their parents, the members of the younger generation embrace the moment with the hectic gaiety of the Roaring Twenties. The teenagers depicted in *Disorder and Early Sorrow* are typical of a certain social set, but decidedly untypical of the average German citizen of the time: they live in palatial homes with servants, telephone frequently, and play records on the gramophone, all signs of conspicuous consumption among the social elite. One of their friends has a father who makes his money speculating on the stock market; he drives a fancy car and throws parties with free champagne. In contrast with the stiff social decorum of prewar society, the young people dress eccentrically and address each other with the familiar "du" as they dance to Afro-Shimmies, Java dances, and Polka Creolas. Boys dance with girls, girls dance with other girls, and some boys even dance with other boys, adding a piquant touch of sexual experimentation to the generally decadent atmosphere of a posh set gone slumming to the "wild, unfamiliar rhythm" of a "monotonous Negro programme" (*aufgeputztes Neger-Amüsement*) (p. 204) – this is the Jazz Age, after all, the time of Josephine Baker. Even the servants no longer know their place: Fräulein Cäcelia, fallen from the middle class to her current role as one of several servants, clings to her past dignity and refuses to wear a cap or any sort of livery that would identify her new role, while the young butler, Xaver Kleinsgütl, is a charming but unreliable "revolutionary servant, a sympathetic Bolshevist," and thus "a child and offspring of dissolute times."

Disorder and Early Sorrow depicts a social order teetering on the brink of chaos, but one that has also unleashed new creative energies. Professor Cornelius observes the younger generation with a combination of detached bemusement and mild concern. In *Mario and the Magician*, however, the mood has grown considerably darker. As in the case of *Death in Venice*, the novella had its origins in an actual event: in the late summer of 1926, Mann had vacationed with his family in Italy, where Mussolini and his Fascist Party had been in power since 1921. In a letter to Gerhardt Hauptmann of September 7, 1926, Mann referred to certain "unpleasant incidents" resulting from the "xenophobic mood of the current national character," although he insisted that otherwise the Italians were as lovable as ever. Three years later while vacationing far to the north in a resort on the Baltic Sea in what was then east Prussia (near Kaliningrad today), Mann decided to base a novella on these events – just as he had once conjured up the north German atmosphere of the Buddenbrooks in Lübeck while living as a young man in Italy.

Told from the perspective of a German gentleman on holiday with his family in Italy, *Mario and the Magician* begins with a description of a vacation gone awry: the weather is hot and sticky, and the Italians make it clear that foreign visitors are unwelcome. Against his better judgment, the narrator nevertheless decides to stay and reluctantly agrees to treat his young children to a late-evening performance by a magician who goes by the name of Cavaliere Cipolla. The chain-smoking charlatan puts on a performance that consists largely of making members of the audience act against their will: he forces a young man to stick out his tongue and then to double over as if in pain; he compels the audience to dance and finally provokes a young man named

Mario to kiss him while hypnotized, having deluded him to think that he is kissing his girlfriend. When Cipolla cracks his whip and Mario realizes what he has done, he shoots and kills the magician.

Mario and the Magician is most obviously an indictment of Italian fascism. The opening pages of the novella depict an otherwise appealing people grown ugly through an exaggerated pride in their own culture and intolerance for others. The series of unpleasant incidents that make the family feel unwanted culminate in a seemingly innocent event that has unexpectedly serious consequences: their little girl undresses to rinse out her bathing suit on the beach and the Italian authorities fine the parents for what they perceive as a shocking breach of public decorum. From the narrator's perspective, however, it is the Italian officials who behave outrageously, turning a trivial incident into a criminal offense. The episode underscores the prudishness that would be typical of German fascism as well. In the above-mentioned essay on "Marriage in Transition," Mann observed that the formerly strict lines between gender roles were becoming blurred in modern Germany, as reflected in Hans Castorp's refusal to challenge his rival in *The Magic Mountain* and in the unconventional behavior of the teenagers in *Disorder and Early Sorrow*. When asked to condemn Klaus Mann's supposedly decadent fiction, Thomas Mann refused, stating that he was no schoolgirl (*Stiftsfräulein*), just as he had earlier defended Paul Verlaine's homoerotic poetry and Frank Wedekind's depictions of adolescent sexuality. German and Italian fascists, in contrast, coupled their drive for a militant nationalism with a backlash against sexual permissiveness, insisting that the "natural" division of labor between the sexes should be restored. From this perspective, the seemingly trivial episode with the naked child on the beach engages directly with the cultural and sexual politics of the time.

The performance itself can be viewed as a fictional representation of the symbiotic relationship established between a charismatic leader and his followers. As Cipolla argues, freedom exists and the will exists, but freedom of the will does not. He works as a hypnotist who compels the people to do his bidding – but at the same time, they are all too willing to let their will be broken, if such a paradoxical statement can be allowed. Commanding and obeying are two sides of the same coin, proclaims Cipolla; *Volk* and *Führer* together make up the unified body of the nation. Also typical of fascism is the association of politics with performance, in keeping with what Walter Benjamin referred to as the "aestheticization of politics." The otherwise tawdry show by a second-rate huckster becomes a metaphor for the political practice of Italian fascism.

Although Mann writes overtly of Italy, he also makes implicit reference to the growing threat of German National Socialism. To be sure, Goebbels was not yet the Minister of Propaganda, who would choreograph the Nazi performances of power, but Hitler was already seducing millions on the national stage. From this perspective, the role of the narrator in *Mario and the Magician* is of particular importance. Mann portrays him as a cultivated northern European who regards the Italians with a mixture of condescension and disapproval, but who is also unable to resist the temptation to witness the performance. Susan Sontag referred to the illicit thrill of the forbidden in her essay on "fascinating fascism"; the narrator falls into the role of the seduced observer, excusing his attendance at the performance as a favor to his children, but staying against his better judgment until the bitter end.

Although *Mario and the Magician* reflects the specific political situation that Mann experienced in the late 1920s, it also conforms to patterns that recur throughout his fiction. In multiple senses, *Mario and the Magician* is the story of a descent to the underworld, a forbidden journey into the heart of darkness. The experience of collective hypnosis most directly recalls Hans Castorp's reluctant participation in Dr. Krokowski's séance, which he ultimately rejects as an unnatural effort to resurrect the dead. Attendance at the performance by the well-to-do German family also marks a step down in terms of social class: Cipolla performs in one of the poorest quarters of the city and appeals most directly to the illiterate members of the lower classes, recalling a pattern of downward social mobility common to the Joker, Tonio Kröger, and the Buddenbrooks. As elsewhere in Mann's fiction, the symbolic descent to the underworld is also associated with the incursion of destructive forces from the east or south. In *Death and Venice* the cholera comes from India; in *Mario and the Magician*, the threat comes from Africa. The heat in the city is explicitly labeled as African, a scirocco that grips the inhabitants in its enervating thrall; the fashionable hairstyle of a fascist nationalist in the audience is also described as African. Mut-em-enet enlists the aid of Tabubu's black magic in the effort to seduce Joseph; here, fascism is linked to blackness as well. The seemingly harmless "African shimmies" danced by Professor Cornelius' teenage children recur in more sinister form in the dances that Cavaliere Cipolla demands of his audience.

While the reader's initial impulse is to identify the voice of the narrator with that of Thomas Mann, other details suggest his secret affinity with Cipolla. Mann's children referred to their father as "the magician" (*der Zauberer*), and he, too, was a public performer. Cipolla is physically handicapped, with a limp and a hunchback, and yet prides himself on having won "the respectful appreciation of the educated public," just as Klaus Heinrich in *Royal Highness* is able to win the hearts of his people despite his withered arm and shy demeanor, both of which can be read as reflections of Mann's own effort to maintain his sense of distinction despite feeling multiply stigmatized. The symbiotic relationship between the performer and his audience in *Mario and the Magician* can be seen as a sinister variant on Mann's self-understanding as a seismograph, as a representative writer whose personal psyche reverberates in tandem with that of the general public. The audience's appreciation of Cipolla's facility with language is said to be typically Italian, recalling Settembrini's precisely articulated pronunciation, yet it is also a gift that Mann shared.

To be part of the Mann family was to share a private language. In his youth, Mann used the term "gippern" to refer to his use of a playfully idiosyncratic slang with Heinrich and his more intimate friends; later visitors to the Mann family noted that they spoke in an affected, precious way to one another, as do the twins in *Wälsungenblut* and the teenagers in *Disorder and Early Sorrow*. Language could work to advance understanding, but it could also be used as a weapon or a tool of seduction, and *Mario and the Magician* captures that sense of danger conveyed by an all-too-glib facility with words. Finally, *Mario and the Magician* culminates in a public exposure of homosexuality, as Mario is compelled to kiss the magician who has insulted him by calling him a "Ganymede," the cup-bearer to the gods in Greek mythology, but also a codeword for homosexuals. In sum, fascism in *Mario and the Magician* appears as a *Heimsuchung*, a visitation of destructive forces that are associatively linked to hypnosis, class degradation, an African invasion of Europe, and an exposure of repressed homosexuality. Thus Mann interprets the new political phenomenon of Italian fascism in terms of his old symbolic vocabulary – a pattern that recurs in *Doctor Faustus*.

Lotte in Weimar

In early October 1936, Thomas Mann began preparations for what he thought would be a short story about Goethe. He had completed *Joseph in Egypt* in August and felt the need for a change of pace before tackling the final volume of *Joseph and his Brothers*. Before long, however, the planned novella had grown into a full-length novel, and it was not until October 26, 1939 that Mann was able to note in his diary that he had completed *Lotte in Weimar*. The novel was written against the backdrop of dramatic political events: Germany annexed Austria in March 1938, occupied the Sudetenland in September, and invaded Poland a year later, precipitating the Second World War. Mann's German citizenship was revoked two months after he began *Lotte in Weimar*, and by the time he finished he had taken up permanent residence in the United States. Work on the project was interrupted by essays on Schopenhauer, Goethe's *Faust*, and Wagner's Ring cycle, as well as dozens of statements and speeches in response to current events; Mann's biographer Hermann Kurzke notes that Mann made over 300 interventions into contemporary politics during the war years, far more than any other member of the exile community.[7] As Mann embarked on extensive lecture tours and sailed back and forth across the Atlantic, the manuscript traveled with him. Mann began *Lotte in Weimar* in Switzerland, continued it in various places, including Sweden, Rhode Island, and on the beach in Holland, before finishing it in Princeton, New Jersey. "At noon today the English ultimatum expired," wrote Mann on September 3, 1939, "from this hour on England and France are at war with Germany. I wrote my page as usual, aware of the events."

As was the case with *Joseph and his Brothers*, *Lotte in Weimar* was both a refuge from swirling political developments and an oblique response to them. In the first instance, the novel is a work of historical fiction, focusing on a meeting between Goethe and Charlotte Kestner, née Buff, in September 1816. The premise of the novel presupposes knowledge of Goethe's early career that would have been familiar to any educated German at the time: after finishing his law degree in Strasburg, Goethe began work in the town of Wetzlar, not far north of his native Frankfurt am Main. There Goethe became interested in Charlotte Buff, who was already engaged to Johann Christian Kestner. An awkward love triangle developed, until Goethe finally broke off the affair and returned to Frankfurt. There he read about the suicide of Karl Wilhelm Jerusalem, an acquaintance from his four months in Wetzlar, which provided the spark for Goethe's first novel, *Die Leiden des jungen Werther* (*The Sorrows of Young Werther*, 1774). The sensationally successful novel tells of a love triangle between the eponymous hero, a fictional character named Charlotte (Lotte for short), and her fiancé; unlike Goethe, however, Werther commits suicide in a way that is directly modeled on Jerusalem's death.

Mann's *Lotte in Weimar* takes place more than four decades after these events. Lotte is now a sixty-three-year-old widow and mother of nine surviving children who has come to Weimar to visit her sister. Goethe is sixty-seven, a world-famous writer and a high-ranking dignitary in Weimar society. Lotte hopes to introduce him to her daughter and sends him a note to let him know that she is in town. She takes up residence at the famous Hotel Elephant, which is still in business today, and meets with a series of individuals who have some sort of connection to the master: the sycophantic innkeeper Mager, a longtime Goethe fan who is overwhelmed to have the "real" Lotte staying at his hotel; Rose Cuzzle, an Irish celebrity hound who travels Europe collecting autographs; Doctor Friedrich Wilhelm Riemer, Goethe's secretary and traveling companion; and Adele Schopenhauer, the sister of the philosopher and close friend of Ottilie von Pogwisch, who is engaged to Goethe's son August. The seventh chapter takes place entirely in Goethe's mind in a stream of conscious-ness that Mann assembled from countless quotations from Goethe's works. Lotte is finally reunited with Goethe during an awkward dinner party in which she finds him aloof and self-absorbed. They meet again in Goethe's carriage outside the Weimar theater for a final conversation that may in fact take place only in Lotte's imagination, and the novel comes to a close.

Lotte in Weimar was hailed as the literary event of the year when it appeared in English translation in 1940, but today's readers may find it a bit of a bore. Nothing happens, or at least nothing that compares with the dramatic events and overwhelming passion of Goethe's *Werther*. Those who read the work in translation will miss the constant stream of allusions to and partial quotations from Goethe's work, and even most German readers today are unlikely to be as versed in the details of Goethe's biography as were those of earlier generations. The novel nevertheless deserves a closer look than many have been willing to give it, both for the subtlety of its psychological portraits and for the insight it grants into Mann's creative process and his contemporary politics.

In a certain sense, *Lotte in Weimar* is a work of unparalleled hubris, as Mann identifies himself with Germany's most famous writer. Goethe's status in German culture cannot be overestimated: Goethe burst onto the literary scene in the early 1770s and went on to define an era through more than sixty years of creative evolution. After his death in 1832, Goethe, together with his friend and rival Schiller, was elevated to the status of a secular saint who was revered as the representative of a nation that prided itself on its achievements in poetry and philosophy. Thomas Mann, who had a detailed knowledge of Goethe's life and works and wrote several substantial essays about him, undertakes an audacious double project in *Lotte in Weimar*: first, to provide an intimate por-trait of a cultural icon, both as he was seen by his contemporaries and how he saw them; and second, to write a fictional autobiography placing himself behind the mask of Goethe.

Many of the statements about Goethe in the novel could apply equally well to Thomas Mann. Goethe had little formal education and was largely self-taught, sometimes masking ignorance with charm. Goethe can get overly dramatic when he reads aloud, but comic scenes leave his audience in stitches. Goethe thinks works through long before he writes them down, and thus they require little or no revision, just as Mann published two segments of *Lotte in Weimar* long before the novel was complete. The actual writing out of the literary works depends more on diligence and patience than inspiration; "it sticks stoutly and unremittingly, through long periods of time, to its task of spinning its web."[8] Young people can have flashes of genius, but the source of mature greatness lies in endurance, in the heroic will to live on despite adversity. Paraphrasing ideas that he had used to describe his own creative process more than thirty years earlier, Mann writes of Goethe's genius as a delicate balancing act, a "just barely possible" dance on the brink of destruction (p. 325). Also important is the understanding of the artist as a parasite that sucks the life out of individuals that he needs for his art. Thus Lotte has suffered throughout her life under the burden of comparisons with her fictional counterpart, just as Mann's "victims" included his Uncle Friedel (Christian Buddenbrook), Gerhardt Hauptmann (Mynheer Peeperkorn), and Gustav Mahler (Gustav von Aschenbach). Lotte is appalled by the sense that Goethe is a god surrounded by the burned flesh of his sacrificial victims, but Goethe insists in their final conversation that he is in fact the biggest victim, tormented by the burden of his genius in a way that is all too familiar to readers of *Tonio Kröger* and *Death in Venice*.

Mann's effort to identify with Goethe in what he half-seriously termed an "unio mystica with the father"[9] is an effort to lend – some might say arrogate – the authority of the master to his own work. In all fairness, there was some justification for the comparison, as Mann was at the zenith of his international fame and a widely acknowledged spokesman for the German émigré community. Mann's imaginative identification with Goethe was also tied to notions of myth that he had explored in *The Stories of Jacob*, in which he characterizes Joseph's father as someone whose sense of personal identity is "open to the past," whose memories of his ancestors replace his sense of a unique identity with the feeling that he is merely repeating mythic patterns. The older Goethe used the term "repeated reflections" (*wiederholte Spiegelungen*) to describe life experience as a palimpsest of memories that accrue over time and eventually seem repetitions and variations of each other. Mann plays on this notion in *Lotte in Weimar*, as Lotte's encounter with August von Goethe is in a sense a repetition of her youthful passion for his father. August's marriage with Ottilie von Pogwisch is a variation of Goethe's infatuation with Lotte, and Goethe's most recent love for the much younger Marianne von Willemer is also a repetition of his earlier love for Lotte.

The setting of the novel in 1816 allows Mann to comment indirectly on the political situation in which he was writing. In October 1806, Napoleon's troops won decisive battles in Jena and Auerstedt. French troops plundered Weimar in the wake of the battle, and in the confusion, Goethe married his long-term mistress, Christiane Vulpius. Polite Weimar society disapproved of Goethe's marriage to an uneducated woman of the lower classes, but Johanna Schopenhauer, the mother of Adele and Arthur and a significant novelist in her own right, welcomed Goethe into her salon. As Adele recalls in *Lotte in Weimar*, Goethe dominated the gatherings by force of his personality. In the course of the next six years, nationalist sentiment against the occupying French forces grew in Germany. In chapter six of *Lotte in Weimar* Adele tells a long story about how she and Ottilie von Pogwisch had cared for a handsome young Prussian soldier wounded in the battle against the French. Adele feels that the young man would be a better match for her friend than August, Goethe's hard-drinking dullard of a son, but Ottilie is resolved to do what she feels is her duty. Incidentally, the tense relations between Goethe and his son in *Lotte in Weimar* closely mirror those between Thomas Mann and his son Klaus. In the end, the Prussian-led German troops defeated Napoleon, entering Paris in May 1814, and then – after Napoleon had escaped from exile on the island of Elba to resume his reign – joining with the British to defeat him for good at the battle of Waterloo in June of the following year.

In the course of the nineteenth century these "Wars of Liberation" attained near mythic status in German history; as Adele Schopenhauer comments sarcastically in chapter five, Napoleon managed to transform even a cosmopolitan humanist such as Wilhelm von Humboldt into a German patriot. Goethe stands alone in his rejection of German nationalism. Goethe admired Napoleon, whom he had met in 1808, and is horrified by the current upsurge of enmity toward the French in the name of German nationalism, "because they are the first manifestation, as yet quite high-minded and harmless, of something frightful, to be displayed some day by us Germans in the form of the crassest follies" (p. 161). Advancing an argument that Mann often used in his denunciations of the National Socialists, Goethe declares that the Germans should stop trying to isolate themselves from the world, but rather open themselves up to it; rather than trying to eradicate internal diversity and conquer Europe, the Germans should abandon bigotry and welcome foreign influences. Practicing what he preaches, Goethe is in the early stages of writing his *West-eastern Divan* (*West-östlicher Divan*, 1819), a cycle of poetry inspired by recent translations from the Persian. Whereas Mann had ridiculed the effeminate French armies during a brief period of machismo at the outbreak of the First World War, he now makes Goethe the spokesman for an "androgynous art" that is simultaneously receptive and productive. "So should Germans be," Mann's Goethe continues, "world-receiving, world-giving, hearts wide open to admire and be fructified," rather than wallowing in a "pig-headed craving to be a unique nation, this national narcissism that wants to make its own stupidity a pattern and power over the rest of the world!" (p. 338). Under such circumstances, maintains Goethe/Mann, the isolated cosmopolitan individual preserves the true spirit of Germany better than the rabidly nationalist majority: "They think they are Germany – but I am. Let the rest perish root and branch, it will survive in me" (p. 331).

In keeping with his argument that the real Germany is to be found among the exiles, Mann's Goethe suggests that the Germans should be scattered abroad like the diasporic Jews. To identify what is best in Germany with the Jews at a time when the Nazis were embarked on a program of persecution that would culminate in the Holocaust was a provocative act. Goethe claims that the Jews are wise and skeptical rather than full of pathos and heroism, and notes their talent for music, medicine, and literature – all virtues, from Mann's anti-Nazi perspective in the late 1930s. Mann is on shakier ground when he has Goethe maintain that the Germans are like the Jews in that they are hated by everyone else, as he risks giving the Germans victim status at a time when they were victimizing others to an unprecedented degree. The primary thrust of the argument that he places in Goethe's mouth, however, is to condemn Germany's militant and xenophobic nationalism in the name of cosmopolitan tolerance – to the point, in fact, that Germany should cease to exist as a political entity and be preserved only in exiles such as Thomas Mann and Goethe, wandering the world divorced of their physical country, but steeped in the spirit of a better Germany.

Transposed Heads and *The Tables of the Law*

After completing *Lotte in Weimar* in late October 1939, Mann was still not ready to return to *Joseph and his Brothers*. On November 12 he noted in his diary that he was reading Heinrich Zimmer's little book about Kali, the mother of the world in Indian mythology, as well as his *Maya: Der indische Mythos* (1939). He began thinking about a new novella based on a motif that he found in Zimmer's work, and on January 5, 1940, Mann began writing his "Indian curiosity." Although Mann repeatedly downplayed the importance of his "divertissement and intermezzo,"[10] it nevertheless occupied him for months. He completed *Transposed Heads: An Indian Legend* (*Die vertauschten Köpfe: eine indische Legende*) in early August, whereupon he returned to the final volume of the Joseph tetralogy.

For a writer most famous for realistic fiction set in modern Europe, *Transposed Heads* marked a significant change of pace. To be sure, *Joseph and his Brothers* is also set in a foreign world in the distant past, but the topic is central to the Judeo-Christian tradition, whereas Mann's playful retelling of an Indian myth seems at first glance utterly alien to his *oeuvre*. As if to stress its anomalous place in his work, Mann referred to it in his diary entry of January 28, 1940 as his "first approach to the French Surrealist sphere" with a reference to Jean Cocteau, whom he knew through Cocteau's friendship with Klaus. Upon closer inspection, however, we find that the novella is not so alien after all, as beneath the Indian masquerade lie themes that are in fact central to Mann's work as a whole.

Transposed Heads tells of two young friends who stumble on a pretty naked girl taking a bath. Schridaman is inflamed with desire and declares that he cannot live without the beautiful Sita, and his friend Nanda, who knows Sita from childhood, agrees to approach her father on his friend's behalf. The father consents and Schridaman marries Sita. Six months later the three set off on a journey, and Sita finds that she is physically attracted to Nanda. They stop at a temple of Kali, the "dark mother" of Indian mythology. Schridaman goes in first and the terrible image of the goddess inspires him to cut off his own head with his sword – which is not easy to do, as the narrator wryly comments. Nanda goes in to look for his friend and ends up cutting off his own head as well. Finally Sita enters the temple, where she finds the decapitated bodies. Obeying the commands of the goddess, Sita reattaches the heads, but in her haste she makes a mistake: Schridaman now has Nanda's body, and vice versa. To whom or what is Sita married? Head or body? They eventually decide that they can never resolve the love triangle, so the two men stab each other in the heart and Sita is burned alive on their funeral pyre – a painful experience, no doubt, as the narrator cheerfully observes, but one that promises Sita the joy of an eternal reunion with her two lovers. Her son survives and becomes a high-ranking servant to the king.

Like the tales of Jacob and Joseph, *Transposed Heads* is another story about death and rebirth, a descent to the womb and tomb of the mythical mother from whom all life emerges and to which all life returns. Behind the veil of Indian mythology lie multiple influences from Western literature and philosophy: Faust's descent to the Mothers in Goethe's drama; Schopenhauer's notion of the Will, which was directly influenced by Hindu thought; Bachofen's description of the matriarchy as an earlier phase of patriarchal society; and Carl Gustav Jung's description of the archetypal hero who renews the world and conquers death by descending to and ascending from the symbolic realm of the mother. *Transposed Heads* also revisits the theme of mind versus body present in Mann's early fiction: Schridaman is an upper-caste articulate intellectual with a flabby body, whereas Nanda has a beautiful body and not much of a mind – recalling an opposition as old as that between Tonio Kröger and Hans Hansen. In keeping with Mann's usual attention to racial difference, Schridaman has considerably lighter skin than his darkly handsome friend. In this case, however, the friendship and rivalry between the two men takes place through the medium of the woman whom they both desire, making *Transposed Heads* a good example of the sort of homoerotic

triangle that Eve Sedgwick has identified as typical of modern gender relations.[11] On the surface, Sita seems an innocent object of male desire, but she
is also a manifestation of the terrible goddess who represents the eternal process of creation and destruction beneath the deceptive surface of transitory
appearances (Maya). As such, Sita is another femme fatale who causes the
death of her two lovers, following a pattern in Mann's work that extends from
Little Herr Friedemann to the horrible cannibalistic hags that Hans Castorp
sees in his vision in the snow.

Transposed Heads is also about the disconnection between mind and body,
about mental adultery, having sex with one person while thinking of another.
Mann had explored this theme in the story of Jacob, who is tricked by Laban
into spending his first wedding night with a woman he thinks is his beloved
Rachel, only to discover in the morning that he has been sleeping with Leah.
Mann was familiar with the theme from Goethe's *Elective Affinities*, a novel in
which a man has sex with his wife while thinking about a younger woman; his
wife gives birth to a child who miraculously resembles the imaginary lover.
The theme also had personal resonance for Mann, whose fifty years of marital monogamy were accompanied by constant homosexual fantasies. Related
to these tales about the indirections of desire – Sita sleeps with her husband's
head but his friend's body – is the related theme of surrogate wooing that will
recur in *Doctor Faustus*: Schridaman desires Sita but sends his friend Nanda
rather than approaching her directly; Sita marries Schridaman, but desires
Nanda. Their differences are reconciled only in death. Although narrated in
a jocular tone, *Transposed Heads* is thus at heart a tragic tale of unrealized
desires and destructive passions.

Mann wrote *The Tables of the Law* between January and March 1943. It was a
commissioned work of wartime propaganda, the first story of ten in an anthol-
ogy organized by Armin L. Robinson, a literary agent who wanted to demon-
strate the evil consequences of a civilization that had reverted to barbarism.
Each of the authors was supposed to choose one of the Ten Commandments
as a central theme, and although Mann's novella quickly grew into a psychological portrait of Moses rather than an illustration of a particular commandment, it was originally published in English translation under the title of the
first commandment: "Thou Shalt Have No Other Gods Before Me" (1943). In
keeping with the initial didactic intent, Mann ends *The Tables of the Law* with
an impassioned curse on those who ignore God's commandments, a passage
that he used verbatim in one of his radio addresses to the German people.

Mann's primary source for *The Tables of the Law* was, of course, the story
of Moses in the book of *Exodus* in the Old Testament, but he was also influenced by Freud's late work, *Moses and Monotheism* (*Der Mann Moses und die*

monotheistische Religion, 1939). Freud had made the controversial suggestion that the Jewish patriarch was in fact an Egyptian who had discovered monotheism at the court of Akhnaton (the same pharaoh that Mann portrays in *Joseph and his Brothers*). Freud speculates that Moses brought monotheism to the Hebrews when he realized that Akhnaton's new religion would not prevail in Egypt. In Thomas Mann's version of the story, Moses is neither an Egyptian nor a Hebrew, but a combination of the two: one day Pharaoh's second daughter sees a Hebrew slave toiling in the sun. She beckons him to her, sleeps with him, and then has him murdered. When she gives birth to a son nine months later, she pretends to have found the child in a wicker basket. The child is raised by a Levite family, but later educated as an Egyptian in Upper Egypt. There young Moses kills an Egyptian and has to flee across the Sinai desert to Midian, where he marries Ziporah.

Like Tonio Kröger and Gustav von Aschenbach, Mann's Moses is an ethnic and cultural hybrid: conceived in a moment of passion between Pharaoh's daughter and an obedient slave, raised as an adopted Hebrew and illegitimate Egyptian, influenced by both cultures, but fully at home in neither. As a result, the Hebrews find him useful in their revolt against the Egyptians, since he can speak both languages and they know that Pharaoh would not dare kill his daughter's child. In addition to his role as a political mediator, Moses must find a way to strike a personal balance between his violent passions and his desire for control. He killed a man in a fit of rage as a young man, writes Mann at the beginning of the novella, and thus he knew better than most that while the act of killing can bring momentary satisfaction, the knowledge that one has killed is a terrible thing and that killing should therefore be forbidden. Moses was also a man of strong sexual desires who kept a mistress in addition to his wife, Mann continues, and thus he desired what was pure and holy. In his role as the leader of the Hebrews, finally, Moses extends his quest for self-discipline to the community, as he imposes order on the unruly mob by writing the laws that form the basis of their future civilization.

Mann's choice of a Jewish patriarch for his implicit critique of Nazi barbarism can be construed as a gesture of philo-Semitic solidarity, as could his positive portrait of Joseph as the benevolent ruler of Egypt. The reaction of Mann's contemporary Jewish readers to *The Tables of the Law* was nevertheless mixed; Mann was astonished when one critic characterized his novella as an "outbreak of hatred against the Jews."[12] Mann protested that he had intended no harm and that he had merely attempted to provide a psychologically plausible portrait of the biblical character, but some readers found his image of Moses as a murderous philanderer with dictatorial inclinations difficult to accept. The very suggestion that the leader of the Hebrews was the bastard child of an Egyptian princess seemed calculated to offend orthodox Jews and literal-minded Christians alike. Those seeking to heap ashes on Mann's head could add the charges of misogyny and racism to that of clandestine anti-Semitism: the source of Moses' inclination toward evil lies in the "looseness and empty pride of his mother's side,"[13] and he chooses as his mistress a Moorish woman from the land of Kush, "a splendid piece of flesh, with towering breasts and rolling whites to her eyes; she had pouting lips, wherein to sink in a kiss might be an adventure to any man" (p. 44). Mann's condemnation of Nazi barbarism here and elsewhere is clear, but by associating the forces of chaos with female sexuality and blackness he opens his own work to charges of prejudice even as he wages war on the bigotry of others.

Chapter 6

A pact with the devil: *Doctor Faustus*

While it is usually possible to reconstruct the origins of Mann's works from his diaries, letters, and essays, he made it easy for us in the case of *Doctor Faustus*, for shortly after completing the novel in 1947 he wrote the "novel of a novel" (*Roman eines Romans*) about the "genesis of Doctor Faustus" (*Die Entstehung des Doktor Faustus*, translated as *The Story of a Novel*). The long essay was originally conceived as something of a preemptive strike: Mann had already come under fire from Arnold Schoenberg for having borrowed his twelve-tone method of composition for his protagonist without permission, and he worried that Theodor Adorno might also protest that he had received insufficient credit for his substantial contributions to the novel, both in helping Mann create plausible descriptions of imaginary compositions and in the theoretical discussions of modern music that Mann included in his work. Thus in *The Story of a Novel* Mann pays tribute to Adorno and acknowledges his contributions to the text – so much so, in fact, that after listening to Mann's reading of the essay's first draft, Katia and Erika insisted that he tone down some of his praise lest he give the impression that Adorno was a coauthor of his work. Taken on its own terms, *The Story of a Novel* is also a highly readable autobiographical account of the years between 1943 and 1947.

In the years prior to *Doctor Faustus*, Mann had split his writing between direct interventions into political events and fictional works set in ancient Egypt, India, or nineteenth-century Weimar that had only an oblique relation to current affairs. In *Doctor Faustus*, in contrast, Mann set out to write "nothing less than the novel of my era," a fictional coming-to-terms with Germany's catastrophic history.[1] Mann viewed it as his *Parsifal*, in a reference to Wagner's last opera, a crowning summation of his life's work and quite possibly his last novel – although he was wrong about this, just as he did not die, as he had once predicted he would, in 1945. Mann begins *The Story of a Novel* with an amusing anecdote about a reporter who visited him in December of that year and was tactless enough to ask him how, in the light of his prediction, he could justify to the public that he was still alive. Mann actually came closer to dying than he knew while writing *Doctor Faustus*, as he was never told that the

101

emergency operation performed by leading surgeons in Chicago in April 1946 was for lung cancer. Against all odds, Mann made a full recovery and was able to complete the novel early the next year. He was convinced that the psycho-logical strain of writing *Doctor Faustus* had contributed to his physical illness. In response to Helen Lowe-Porter's comment that he had given his "utmost to the German people" with this novel, Mann wrote that "all art which deserves the name testifies to this determination to reach the ultimate, this resolve to go to the limits" (*The Story of a Novel*, p. 158).

Mann began work on *Doctor Faustus* almost immediately after having com-pleted *The Tables of the Law* in March 1943, but the origins of the project went back almost forty years. "Thoughts of an old plan for a novella 'Dr. Faust,'" Mann noted in his diary on March 14. The reference was to a brief diary entry of around 1904,[2] in which Mann jots down an idea about a syphilitic artist whose creative powers are temporarily heightened by the disease, but who is taken by the devil in the end. In its core, therefore, *Doctor Faustus* is another variant on the romantic theme of genius heightened by disease that Mann had already explored in *Death in Venice* and *The Magic Mountain*. In *Doctor Faus-tus* the protagonist, Adrian Leverkühn, is an avant-garde composer who con-tracts syphilis with an infected prostitute. The illness grants him intermittent bursts of creative genius over a twenty-four-year period before he succumbs to mental illness.

The novel takes the form of a fictional biography, written by Leverkühn's boyhood friend Serenus Zeitblom, as indicated by the novel's somewhat bar-oque subtitle: *The Life of the German Composer Adrian Leverkühn as told by a Friend* (*Das Leben des deutschen Tonsetzers Adrian Leverkühn erzählt von einem Freunde*). *Doctor Faustus* can also be regarded as a tragic variant of the *Bildungsroman*, as the development of the protagonist leads initially to per-sonal maturation and artistic achievement, but ends in alienation from society, unrequited love, madness, and death. Leverkühn is born in 1885 on a farm outside of Weissenfels, a medium-sized city in Saxony. He has a blond, typ-ically German father who looks like he has walked out of an Albrecht Dürer painting, and a dark-haired mother with a musical voice who could almost be mistaken for an Italian – Tonio Kröger and Gustav von Aschenbach all over again. When he is ten, Leverkühn moves to the fictive town of Kaisersaschern, about forty-five minutes by train from his parents' farmstead. There he attends school while living in the home of his uncle, Nikolaus Leverkühn, a violin-maker and seller of musical instruments. Leverkühn learns to play piano and makes his first experiments at composition, but he studies theology rather than music when he attends the University of Halle. In 1905, he switches to the University of Leipzig, where he plans to study philosophy, but devotes himself primarily to music under the guidance of his old mentor, Wendell Kretzschmar. Leverkühn later moves to Munich, but soon takes a simple room on a farm in the tiny town of Pfeiffering in Upper Bavaria. There he collapses in a syphilitic fit in 1930; he spends the last decade of his life in his mother's care on the farm where he was born.

Serenus Zeitblom writes the biography of his deceased friend over a two-year period beginning on May 23, 1943. The fact that Mann began writing *Doctor Faustus* on precisely this date according to both his diary entry of that day and *The Story of a Novel* tempts us to identify Mann with Zeitblom, but caution is advised.[3] Zeitblom stops writing at the end of the Second World War; Mann did not complete *Doctor Faustus* until early 1947. Zeitblom is Catholic by birth (Mann was Protestant, as is his protagonist Adrian Leverkühn) and a classical humanist by profession. He teaches for many years at a college preparatory high school (*Gymnasium*), but has gone into early retirement because he "was never able to agree fully" with Hitler's treatment of the Jews and because he does not share his sons' enthusiasm for the Führer.[4] As such, Zeitblom is typical of what became known as "inner emigrants," individuals who disapproved of National Socialism but remained in Germany and did not protest openly, while Mann was a leading member of the exile community who spoke out passionately on a regular basis against Nazi Germany.

Zeitblom is increasingly disturbed by the destruction of the German cities and the damning revelations of the liberated concentration camps, but there are times in his narrative when he cannot repress enthusiasm for the advances in German war technology, and his condemnation of the Nazi persecution of the Jews seems lukewarm at best. Zeitblom knows that there is no audience in wartime Germany for his biography of the avant-garde composer, whose works would surely have been branded "degenerate art," so he writes for what he hopes will be a future audience to appreciate his friend's genius. Zeitblom is proud of his friendship with the reclusive artist and jealous of anyone else, particularly other men, who might win Leverkühn's favor; although Zeitblom has married a woman named Helene out of a sense of duty and because her name reminds him of classical antiquity (Helen of Troy), the work seethes with barely suppressed homosexual tension between the men who vie for Leverkühn's affection.

Although *Doctor Faustus* can be read as a realistic novel about an imaginary artist, it has multiple layers of symbolic depth. Most obviously, it is a retelling of the Faust story, which had its origins in the life of a man who lived from approximately 1480 to 1540. This mysterious intellectual and alchemist became the subject of popular legends in the late sixteenth century, one of which made its way to England in 1588 and became the source of Christopher

Marlowe's tragedy. The legend lived on in popular chapbooks and in the theater until Goethe transformed it into a work of philosophical profundity and lyric beauty that is generally considered the single most important work of German literature. In deciding to write his own version of the Faust story, then, Thomas Mann was once again casting himself in the role of Goethe's heir, measuring his own genius against that of the heavyweight champion of German literature.

There were two further reasons why the Faust theme was a particularly apt choice for Mann's reckoning with German history. First, the figure of Faust had become identified with the German nation in the course of the nineteenth century. As Hans Schwerte demonstrates in his classic study of *Faust und das Faustische* (1962), German writers often flattered themselves by declaring the German national character "Faustian" in its boldness, its reckless willingness to plunge forward, even into death, if necessary – a recklessness reflected in the hysterical outburst of enthusiasm that greeted Joseph Goebbels when he asked his audience of Nazi loyalists in 1943 if they wanted "total war." The second appealing aspect of the Faust legend was that it allowed Mann to extend his focus beyond the fate of Germany to consider that of Western civilization as a whole. Unlike mythical heroes of classical antiquity or the biblical patriarchs, Faust was a modern historical individual who embodied the spirit of the Renaissance in his curiosity about the world, his quest for knowledge, and his desire for powers not sanctioned by the Church. Successive generations of writers from Marlowe to Goethe to Mann adapted this figure as a metaphor for modern Europe, both in its humanist aspirations and in its catastrophic defeats. Thomas Mann's *Doctor Faustus* is not only about the endgame of Nazi Germany, but also about the end of an entire phase of European history that stretches back to the Renaissance.

The original Faust legend is firmly rooted in traditional Christian theology: Faust signs a pact in blood with an emissary of the devil to receive a limited period of heightened powers on earth in return for eternal damnation in hell. Very soon, however, the religious parable was secularized and psychologized. Already in Marlowe, hell has become a state of mind rather than a specific place. Goethe transforms the original still further by making his devil, Mephistopheles, an unwilling ally of God as he spurs Faust to live more intensely in a pantheistic universe. In Thomas Mann's version of the tale, the pact takes the form of having sex with an infected prostitute; Leverkühn gains a limited period of heightened genius, but loses his life in the end. The devil appears to Leverkühn long after he has sealed his fate in a scene that is modeled on Ivan Karamozov's feverish encounter with the devil in Dostoevsky's last novel. Leverkühn describes the experience as if it were real in a letter to

Zeitblom, but there are hints that he suffers a syphilitic hallucination in which the devil takes on three distinct forms: a pimp, in reference to the prostitute who carried the disease; an intellectual who resembles Theodor Adorno; and a theologian, Eberhard Schleppfuss, who had introduced Leverkühn to unorthodox ideas about the necessity of sin during his student days in Halle. Parallel to the romantic theme of artistic genius stimulated by disease is the suggestion that Germany has signed a pact with the devil in the guise of Adolf Hitler and the Nazis, granting it temporary world power, but leading to military defeat and moral corruption.

The Faustian recklessness is reflected in the hero's name – "kühn" means bold and "Lever" is close enough to "Leben" or "life" to suggest that his name means "live boldly." The name thus translated alludes to the philosophy of Friedrich Nietzsche, another genius who succumbed to madness, probably also as a result of a syphilitic infection. Mann used many of the details about Nietzsche's life and his final illness for the character of Adrian Leverkühn; there is also a hint of Nietzschean influence in the name of Leverkühn's musical mentor, Wendell Kretzschmar. Although Nietzsche had no patience for the rampant nationalism in Bismarck's imperial Germany and openly ridiculed anti-Semites, his praise of supermen and blond beasts, blatant misogyny, and ruthless rejection of conventional morality and Christian pity played into the hands of Nazi ideologues. Still another figure behind Mann's protagonist is Martin Luther, the mercurial German monk who dared to challenge the authority of Roman Catholicism. Mann had used Luther as a symbol of Germany as the "protesting nation" in the *Reflections*, the land that refused to align itself with Western Europe. Like Faust and Nietzsche, Luther is another titanic German figure with an ambivalent legacy, famous for his courage and notorious for his capacity for hatred and rage. He appears as a caricature in the novel as one of Leverkühn's theology professors, Ehrenfried Kumpf, who parodies Luther's language and gestures, but in a broader sense the spirit of Luther's early modern Germany lives on in the Saxon and Thuringian cities where Leverkühn spends his formative years.

Faust, Nietzsche, and Luther – in a certain sense, Adrian Leverkühn is all of these, which is to say that he represents Germany. But so did Thomas Mann: "Where I am, there is Kaisersaschern" (p. 242), proclaims Leverkühn in a parodic reference to Mann's famous identification of himself with German culture. In *The Story of a Novel*, Mann refers to *Doctor Faustus* as "a radical confession" (p. 154), and there are in fact many autobiographical elements in the work, beginning with Leverkühn's mixed parents. Mann's description of the fictional city of Kaisersaschern is borrowed verbatim from his description of his hometown in "Lübeck as a Spiritual Form of Life." The artistic and intellectual milieu that Leverkühn experiences in Munich is Mann's own. Frau Senator Rodde closely resembles Mann's mother Julia; her daughters Inez and Clarissa are modeled on Mann's sisters Julia (Lulu) and Carla. Thomas Mann's somewhat parasitic friend Hans Reisiger appears as Leverkühn's companion, Rüdiger Schildknapp; Paul Ehrenberg, the musician whom Mann had loved when he was a young man in Munich, is featured as the virtuoso violinist Rudi Schwerdtfeger; Leverkühn's nephew Nepomuk is modeled on Mann's favorite grandson Frido, and the list goes on. In many ways, *Doctor Faustus* is the continuation of *Buddenbrooks* that Mann never wrote, a fictional autobiography full of thinly veiled portraits of family and friends.

At the same time, Mann distances his work from direct confession through the use of what he called his "montage-technique." The term *montage* comes from the visual arts, referring to a single image that combines materials from various sources, either in a way that foregrounds the disparate origins of the components or that conceals them behind the apparent unity of the new work. Mann uses both techniques in *Doctor Faustus*, sometimes identifying his literary sources – Shakespeare, William Blake, the German writers Klopstock and Kleist – but more often obscuring the reference by making it seem part of the narrative. Mann lists many of his sources in *The Story of a Novel* and scholars have discovered many more.[5] Examples of materials used include passages from Mann's own essays, episodes lifted directly from Nietzsche's biography, discussions about the social significance of avant-garde art in Adorno's *Philosophy of Modern Music*, the preface to a book about butterflies that Hermann Hesse had given to Mann, and an article from *Life* magazine about exploring the ocean depths in a bathysphere.

Although Mann first introduced the term *montage-technique* in *The Story of a Novel*, he had been using variants of the artistic practice since early in his career. Mann routinely incorporated disparate materials into his fiction, usually without acknowledging the source. In some cases Mann was accused of stealing other people's ideas: Arnold Schoenberg insisted that Mann add a footnote to all future editions of *Doctor Faustus* identifying him as the inventor of the twelve-tone or row technique of composition attributed in the novel to Adrian Leverkühn. Aside from raising delicate ethical questions concerning the respective claims of artistic license versus intellectual property rights, Mann's use of the montage-technique affords an interesting look into his creative process. As noted earlier, Mann's overall conception of his novels was fixed long before he finished writing them, allowing him to publish in advance chapters from an uncompleted work. At the same time, however, Mann added new ideas and materials into his fiction as he went along, as he worked on projects that took him several years, or, in the case of *Joseph and his Brothers* and the

Confessions of Felix Krull, decades to complete. When finished, his novels give the impression of careful planning and great erudition, but the actual process of writing depended at least as much on Mann's ability to incorporate serendipitous discoveries and experiences into an overall concept. His scholarly knowledge of any given field went only as deep as he needed it for the purposes of his fiction, whether he was writing about ancient Egypt or modern music. When the job was done, he packed up his materials and moved on to the next project.

Mann's use of the montage-technique in *Doctor Faustus* raises questions about artistic originality and genius that are central to the theoretical portions of the work. As young men in Kaisersaschern, Leverkühn and Zeitblom attend a series of lectures open to the general public about music history and theory delivered by Wendell Kretzschmar. The audiences are tiny, both because Kretzschmar lectures on difficult and obscure topics and because he is afflicted with a bad stutter, but they lay out a theory of cultural development that defines Leverkühn's place in music history. Kretzschmar explains that, in the beginning, all music was composed for the Church, but during the romantic era culture emancipated itself from the religious cult. As the Enlightenment began to erode religious faith and the French Revolution overthrew the political order, artists stepped in to try to make sense of a world that had lost its traditional bearings. The artist was now viewed as an original genius rather than a skilled craftsman and works of art were conceived as autonomous entities to be enjoyed for their own sake, no longer subservient to Church or State. Not coincidentally, the romantic era also gave birth to the institution of the museum as a place where the general public could view works of art previously produced for private patrons. Parallel developments included the emergence of "absolute music" to be played in concert halls rather than in churches or at royal palaces, and professional writers who lived from the profits of their publications rather than the favor of their aristocratic patrons.

Liberation from Church and State also placed a tremendous burden on the artist, who was alone at the helm of a ship cast loose from its traditional political and religious moorings. Kretzschmar's symbol of the modern artist *in extremis* is Beethoven, who emerges looking haggard and haunted from a sleepless night of agonizing struggle with his art; Leverkühn will also be ravaged with grief and exhaustion when he appears for the last time before his former friends and acquaintances. The demand for originality also places a strain on the artist. As the devil explains in his guise as a music theorist, certain musical forms that seemed innovative when first introduced sound hackneyed in the work of subsequent composers. In his early career, Leverkühn feels cursed by the sense that he has come too late, that musical innovation has run its course and that he can only compose by parodying outmoded forms. He longs to break through to a new form of artistic expression that would go beyond the sterility of an exhausted tradition, just as Kretzschmar predicts that the isolation of the romantic artist will eventually end: the individual genius will be reunited with the collective will and culture will return to its cultic function.

Leverkühn does achieve his musical breakthrough by "inventing" the twelve-tone or row technique. Traditional Western music is set in either a major or minor key; in both cases musical scales of seven notes are centered on a key note or tonic. To use an example from popular culture, the note "do" is the tonic of the major scale that Maria (as played by Julie Andrews) teaches the von Trapp children to sing as "Doe, a deer" in *The Sound of Music*. In the early twentieth century, Hindemith and Bartok employed the "major-minor system," in which all twelve notes were grouped around a center or tonic, resulting in an emotionally ambiguous music typical of modern sensibilities. Schoenberg went one step further, rebelling against the "tyranny of the tonic" and deciding to treat all notes equally – the musical equivalent of abandoning the principle of gravity. The resulting compositions were not merely chaotic, however, but organized around a "tone row" or "basic set" that was unique to each piece, rather than in terms of a traditional major or minor key. Variations are possible, as the tone row can begin on any note in the sequence, be played backward and forward, right side up or upside down, but the row itself cannot be altered. The result is a paradoxical combination of utter freedom from the traditional conventions of Western music and utter constraint to the tone row unique to a particular composition. As Leverkühn puts it to Zeitblom, such a work would be "bound by the self-imposed constraint of order, which means free" (p. 207).

The adoption of this technique allows Leverkühn to "break through" the cynical parody of exhausted forms to a new expressiveness in his work. Zeitblom uses the same term in a political sense to characterize Germany's "breakthrough to world power" (p. 324) under Hitler, and he uses the term again to describe young Nazi enthusiasts who see the war as a means by which Germany can break "through to a new form of life in which state and culture would be one" (p. 317) – a formulation that recalls Kretzschmar's prediction of a new era in which culture would regain its cultic function and the isolated genius be reintegrated into the collective. How, then, are we to understand the relationship between Leverkühn's avant-garde art and the politics of National Socialism? Certainly not in any direct sense: Leverkühn is a reclusive cosmopolitan who produces avant-garde art that would not have been permitted in Nazi Germany. He takes no interest in politics during his conscious life and succumbs to his illness already in 1930, three years before Hitler assumed power. Leverkühn is a cold intellectual who is forbidden to love – his attempt to marry Marie Godeau by sending his friend Rudi Schwerdtfeger to propose on his behalf ends in disaster – but a lack of emotional warmth does not necessarily make him or anyone else a Nazi.

Leverkühn's artistic sensibilities are seismographic rather than overtly political; he is mysteriously in touch with the spirit of the age even though – or precisely because – he is not actively involved in daily political affairs. His push forward to a new style is also described as a reversion to pre-civilized barbarism; his mature work combines rigid form with unbridled passion in a way that anticipates the Nazi "aestheticization of politics" in choreographed rallies that combine militarist precision with mass hysteria. Leverkühn becomes a kind of Nietzschean anti-Christ who represents Germany even though he is distanced from it. He describes his final composition as the refutation of Beethoven's Ninth Symphony, declaring an end to all that is good and noble in a work that promises damnation rather than salvation.

According to this logic, Leverkühn is not to blame for what happened in Nazi Germany; he is merely the needle on a cultural seismograph, the highly calibrated instrument that registers the shocks of the impending catastrophe. Who, then, is to blame? Mann offers mixed messages in *Doctor Faustus.* To a certain extent, Mann implies that the blame lies with irresponsible intellectuals who dabble in reactionary ideas without considering the potential political consequences. Two groups in particular stand out: Leverkühn's fellow theology students and members of the "Christian Society Winfried" at the University of Halle, and the group of conservative intellectuals that congregates at evening salons in Munich. The former are callow youths with patriotic names such as Konrad Deutschlin and Carl Teutleben who pontificate about the profundity and "powerful immaturity" (p. 127) of the German soul, the priority of the state over the individual, and the proximity of Germany's instinctual vitality to the demonic. The Munich intellectuals are older and more sinister. They include a reactionary aristocrat, a racist literary historian, a mild-mannered history professor who lisps about blood and passion, a bombastic poet who proclaims world conquest, and Dr. Chaim Breisacher, who mocks the notion of historical progress and predicts that society will soon eliminate those deemed unfit to live in the name of racial hygiene.

At the same time, Mann implicitly absolves these individuals of guilt by suggesting that their beliefs are merely manifestations of deep-seated tendencies in the German soul. Characteristic of this latter view is a fluctuation in *Doctor Faustus* between the understanding of history as chronological progression and timeless stasis. On the one hand, Mann works with two carefully dated chronological sequences in the novel: the events that lead from Leverkühn's birth in 1885 to his death in 1940, and Zeitblom's writing of the biography between 1943 and 1945. On the other hand, Mann repeatedly disrupts the narrative progress to suggest that Nazi barbarism is not radically new, but an eruption of forces that have long been latent within Germany. The town of Kaisersaschern is filled with Gothic and Renaissance architecture that signals continuity with medieval superstitions and a tendency toward mob violence that lie beneath the veneer of modern civilization. Mann's use of disparate source material for the depiction of the Halle theology students reveals a similar tendency to collapse historically distinct moments into a simultaneous present: Mann relied primarily on a long letter from the theologian Paul Tillich to recreate the ambiance of German student life around 1900, but some of the ideas that the students express are borrowed from a right-wing fraternity pamphlet of 1931, while many of the names of the students are taken from Luther's sixteenth-century correspondence. Fashions and language may change superficially, Mann suggests, but the German character remains fundamentally the same.

As Mann was well aware, the suggestion that fascist tendencies lay latent in the German soul could not only absolve individuals of responsibility for their actions, but even "do its part in creating a new German myth, flattering the Germans with their 'demonism'" (*Dämonie*), as he put it in *The Story of a Novel* (p. 55). Subsequent readers have criticized *Doctor Faustus* for precisely this reason, arguing that Mann is complicit with the ideology he condemns, mystifying German "essence" rather than seeking specific economic or political causes for German National Socialism. While Mann was a tireless opponent of Hitler's Germany in his essays and public speeches, no character in the novel corresponds to this role. Zeitblom is isolated, impotent, and at times guilty of enthusiasm for the regime he otherwise condemns; Leverkühn's apolitical music is described as an early artistic manifestation of the spirit of the age that gives birth to National Socialism. The result is to create a sense of fatalism in the novel that contrasts with Mann's political activism in other venues. In life, Mann fights the good fight against German fascism; in retrospect, he referred to the Hitler years as "morally a good era" (*moralisch gute Zeit*) (*The Story of a Novel*, p. 163). In his art, however, Mann suggests that National Socialism was Germany's inevitable destiny.

Still more controversial is Mann's representation of Jewish characters in *Doctor Faustus*. Mann has been accused of committing sins of omission and commission in this regard. Among the former is the absence of anti-Semitism in the proto-fascist discussions in the work. Since Mann lays the blame for German National Socialism on irresponsible intellectuals, why is anti-Semitism missing from the novel when it played such a central role in Nazi ideology? Zeitblom refers to the historically accurate event in which the citizens of Weimar were commanded to walk through the Buchenwald concentration camp and witness the extent of suffering and death that many were still trying to deny, but there is no mention of the fact that most of the victims were Jews. Of the various characters explicitly identified as Jewish in *Doctor Faustus*, two have been singled out for particular attention. One is the impresario Saul Fitelberg, who tries to lure Leverkühn out of his hermit-like isolation by offering to send him on a concert tour and to introduce him to Parisian society. Some of Mann's earliest readers, including his son Klaus, thought that this fast-talking eastern European Jew – who transforms art into money, switches back and forth between German and French, and insinuates himself into high society – could easily be interpreted as an anti-Semitic caricature. More sinister is the Jewish intellectual Dr. Chaim Breisacher, whom Zeitblom describes with unconcealed hatred as one of the most unpleasant "specimens" of his race that he has encountered, a "foreign body" in German society who predicts with fatal accuracy that future societies will soon begin to eliminate those deemed unfit to live.

Why would Thomas Mann, who spoke out repeatedly during the war years against anti-Semitism and the Nazi persecution of the Jews, make the most obnoxious proto-fascist in *Doctor Faustus* a Jew? Mann would argue that he was simply reproducing historical reality: Breisacher is based on Oskar Goldberg, whose book, *The Reality of the Hebrews* (*Die Wirklichkeit der Hebräer*, 1925), Mann had consulted when writing *Joseph and his Brothers*. Goldberg argued that ancient gods were not universal but rather specific to a particular people or race; he viewed civilization and rationality as symptoms of decline and advocated a return to blood sacrifice. Breisacher could therefore be cited as an example of the irony of history: an individual who advocates theories that, when put into practice, will lead to his own destruction. Given Mann's frequent suggestion of the affinity between Jewish intellectuals and modern artists, moreover, there is a certain logic behind his decision to cast the most radical reactionary ideologue in *Doctor Faustus* as a tragically prescient Jew, just as the most uncompromising avant-garde artist composes music that inadvertently and yet inevitably anticipates the coming barbarism. And yet, one might argue, there were plenty of non-Jewish intellectuals who paved the way for German fascism; by highlighting a Jewish proto-fascist, Mann seems to suggest that the Jews are responsible for their own destruction, while his demonization of the German soul works in the opposite direction, not only mitigating German guilt, but even reinforcing flattering myths about their tragic-heroic Faustian nature. Thus *Doctor Faustus* denounces National Socialism even as it perpetuates aspects of the ideology it condemns.

Chapter 7

Tribulations and final triumphs

Mann's last years

The final decade of Mann's life was in some ways a vindication and celebration. Mann had been right about Hitler and the National Socialists, unlike so many of his contemporary Germans, and his efforts against the war and on behalf of world peace were now recognized and rewarded. The University of Bonn returned the honorary doctorate that it had revoked in 1936, the city of Lübeck declared him an honorary citizen, and many more awards and honorary degrees from major European and North American universities followed. Mann was received by heads of state, royalty, and the pope; overflow audiences gave him standing ovations when he spoke, and he was often hailed as the greatest living man of letters. Even death was gentle when it came on August 12, 1955: the writer who had specialized in gruesome depictions of death and dying, from the clinical details of Hanno Buddenbrook's typhoid fever to the excruciating account of Nepomuk Schneidewein's cerebral meningitis, passed away quietly in his hospital bed from complications of arterial sclerosis.

Although Mann took pride in his accomplishments and basked in the recognition he received, his final years were nevertheless neither easy nor happy. "Very tired, nervous, and suffering," Mann noted in his diary on August 14, 1949. "My life is truly *la vie difficile*." Although Mann recovered from his major lung operation in the spring of 1946, there were signs of aging. He fell and fractured a shoulder leaving a dinner party at the home of Max Horkheimer. His teeth and partial dentures caused discomfort and made it difficult for him to eat; in his final years Mann lived on little more than soup and caviar, noting frequently that he was losing weight. Sleep was impossible without a cocktail of sedatives – and this from a man who had once written an essay about how much he enjoyed his rest ("Süßer Schlaf!" [Sweet Sleep!], 1909). Friends and family members began to die, increasing Mann's sense of isolation; within less than a year he lost his younger brother, Viktor, his older brother, Heinrich, and his son, Klaus, who committed suicide in May 1949. Even writing became difficult. Mann looked back with a sigh at the time when he was able to complete one major project after the next. Now, after having completed his magnum opus in *Doctor Faustus*, he felt that his life's work was done, and yet, life without work was inconceivable. So Mann wrote on, but he wrote unhappily, worrying that his work had become dull or frivolous or simply pointless.

Political controversies compounded Mann's personal problems. The Allied victory brought surprisingly little joy, as Mann was convinced that most Germans felt no remorse for what they had done and that all but the worst criminals would be quickly reintegrated into German society, which indeed turned out to be the case. Within months after the Second World War ended the Cold War began, and Mann grew increasingly uncomfortable as his adopted country turned to witch-hunting and red-baiting in the McCarthy era. Mann repeatedly insisted that he was not a communist, but he feared that the struggle against communism would turn American democracy into fascism. Mann followed the proceedings of the House Committee on Un-American Activities with revulsion, and although he was never required to testify, the FBI did assemble a substantial dossier of materials that could have been used against him.

Mann's relations with postwar Germany were equally fraught. Some wanted him to return to Germany as a force of healing, but Mann refused to overlook the hurt and anger caused by his twelve years in exile. Matters got worse when he declared in an open letter of September 7, 1945 that any book published in Germany between 1933 and 1945 was "less than worthless" (conveniently forgetting that the first three Joseph novels appeared in Germany between 1933 and 1936!). "A stench of blood and shame clings to them; they should all be destroyed." Furious authors of the "inner emigration" lashed back, claiming that while they had been suffering the hardships of war, Mann had been living in luxury under California's sunny skies. How dare he proclaim judgment on them now! A few years later Mann stirred up more controversy when he finally did return to Germany and delivered speeches in both the Allied and the Russian occupation zones. Mann insisted that he spoke for all of Germany, despite its current political division, and that it was therefore important to travel to Weimar as well as Frankfurt, but the reconciliatory gesture provoked outrage instead. Did he not realize that his appearance in Weimar legitimated a repressive regime? Did he not know that the communists were using the former concentration camp of Buchenwald to detain political prisoners? Although Mann actually wrote a long letter to General Secretary Walter Ulbricht in June 1951 on behalf of the political prisoners in the German Democratic Republic, the impression remained among many in the Federal Republic and in the United States that he was "soft on communism," if not a "fellow traveler." Increasingly uncomfortable in the United States and unwilling to return to Germany, Mann spent his final years in Switzerland.

The Holy Sinner

In chapter thirty-one of *Doctor Faustus*, Adrian Leverkühn comes across a story titled "The Birth of Saint Gregory the Pope" in a medieval collection of tales known as the *Gesta Romanorum*. Because Leverkühn uses the story for his marionette opera, *Apocalipsis cum figures*, Zeitblom provides a detailed plot summary: according to ancient legend, the twin children of Duke Grimald, Wiligis and Sibylla, find each other so attractive that they crawl into bed together – many times – until Sibylla discovers that she is pregnant. Acting on the advice of a wise old councilor, Sibylla retreats to a remote estate where she has the baby and then puts the infant out to sea. Wiligis sets off on a pilgrimage to the Holy Lands, where he soon dies, and Sibylla vows never to marry. Meanwhile, the boat with the abandoned baby drifts to a remote island, where it is found by two simple fishermen and a monk named Gregorius. The handsome boy grows up on the island under the watchful eye of Gregorius, who names Gregor after himself. At age seventeen, young Gregor discovers that he is not the child of his foster parents and sets sail to discover his true identity.

Fortune brings him to the land of Sibylla, now queen but under siege by a suitor who refuses to take "no" for an answer. Gregor becomes her champion, defeats the rival, and marries his mother. Only after she has had one child and is pregnant with another does Sibylla discover that she has married her own son – who is also her nephew! She vows chastity and Gregor sets off to do penance for his unprecedented sin. A fisherman on an inland sea shackles Gregor to a rocky island and throws the key into the water. Here Gregor spends seventeen years, nourished only by a milky fluid that oozes from the rocks. Then the pope dies in distant Rome. The succession is disputed until two pious old men receive the same vision proclaiming that Gregor is to be the new pope. They set off in search of him and find the fisherman and his wife, who at first deny any knowledge of the man they once abandoned on the island. In the fish that they serve for dinner, however, the fisherman finds the very key that he had once thrown away. He confesses, they row out to the rock, and find that Gregor has miraculously survived. They bring him to Rome, where he becomes a wise and just pope.

After completing *Doctor Faustus*, Mann decided to base a short novel on this story. In preparation, he studied another version of the tale by the German medieval writer Hartmann von Aue with the help of a professor who translated the text into modern German for him. He began writing *Der Erwählte* (literally, "the chosen one," translated as *The Holy Sinner*) in January 1948 and completed it nearly three years later, in October 1950. Readers familiar with the dark world of *Doctor Faustus* and the difficult circumstances of Mann's life during these years might be surprised to discover in *The Holy Sinner* a relentlessly cheerful work that leads to a resoundingly happy ending, narrated in a chipper tone by an Irish monk living in Germany. Mann's decision to follow his tragic novel with a comedy actually fits into a pattern that he followed throughout his career: after tracing the decline of a family in *Buddenbrooks*, he wrote about the marriage of a prince in *Royal Highness*; he left Hans Castorp facing probable death on the battlefields of the First World War, but then followed Joseph's rise from spoiled brat to wise ruler. Like *Joseph and his Brothers*, *The Holy Sinner* was written in deliberate opposition to troubled times. "Ernst ist das Leben, heiter ist die Kunst," wrote Schiller at the end of his prologue to the drama *Wallenstein* that Mann knew so well: "Life is serious, art is cheerful."

But why this particular story? As in the case of *Wälsungenblut* and the story of Potiphar's parents in *Joseph in Egypt*, Mann is drawn to the theme of incest that he knew from the first act of Wagner's *Die Walküre* as well as Freud's essays on the Oedipus complex. In the case of Potiphar's parents, Huya and Tuya, incest is a sign of regression to the primitive practice of undisciplined sexual desire that Bachofen called "unregulated hetaerism." Joseph, in contrast, progresses to the stability of an individual identity typical of Bachofen's patriarchy or Freud's successful resolution of the Oedipus complex. Incest in *The Holy Sinner* is more like the love between Siegmund and Sieglinde Aarenhold in *Wälsungenblut*: Wiligis and Sibylla find themselves so much better than anyone else that they find it natural to sleep only with one another. Their child inherits their innate sense of superiority: although he is raised by simple peasants, he knows that he is not cut from common cloth, and when he compounds the guilty circumstances of his birth by marrying his mother, he commits a sin that is commensurate with his great distinction – "where there is Blemish, there is nobility. Baseness shows no blemish."[1] In this regard, Gregor is like Klaus Heinrich in *Royal Highness*, who is distinguished by his royal birth, but stigmatized by his withered hand. The plot of *The Holy Sinner* follows the pattern of ritual death and symbolic rebirth that is also central to *Joseph and his Brothers*: baby Gregor is set adrift on the "mother-darkness" (*Mutterdunkel*) of the sea (p. 98); the incestuous man is abandoned on the island where he finds sustenance from the "mother's breast" (*Mutterbrust*) (p. 252) of the rock that emits the nourishing milk. In *Transposed Heads*, the descent to the realm of the mother leads to the loss of identity and death for Nanda and Schridaman, but in *Joseph and his Brothers* and *The Holy Sinner* the hero is strengthened by his ordeal and rises to new heights.

Mann's decision to base a novel on the theme of *The Holy Sinner* also raises questions about his attitude toward religion. Mann was baptized as a Lutheran in Lübeck, and he and Katia had their children baptized as Protestants as well. Although Mann was not a practicing Christian, some have noted an increased interest in religion and religious themes in his later work. In his autobiography (*Achterbahn*, 2008), Mann's grandson Frido stresses Thomas Mann's interest in the Unitarian Church in the last decade of his life, while Hermann Kurzke writes of Mann's turn toward a vaguely Christian humanism during these years.[2] The theme of God's grace or mercy (*Gnade*) that is central to *The Holy Sinner* could be seen as the counterpart to the theme of *Heimsuchung*, or the visitation of harmful forces, that also pervades Mann's work: against the fear that the forces of chaos will reach up and destroy the precarious equilibrium of his own life and that of his protagonists is the tenuous hope for mercy, forgiveness, or even salvation. Zeitblom ends *Doctor Faustus* with a prayer for mercy and speaks of the "hope beyond hopelessness, the transcendence of despair" (p. 515) that he thinks he hears in Leverkühn's last composition. *The Magic Mountain* ends with a question: "And out of this worldwide festival of death [...] will love someday rise up out of this, too?" (p. 706). Even *Buddenbrooks* ends not with death but the promise of eternal life from old Sesami Weichbrodt, who, trembling with conviction, proclaims her faith like "an inspired, scolding little prophet" (p. 731). While it may be going too far to read Mann's works as Christian in any dogmatic or orthodox sense of the term, they are deeply rooted within a Judeo-Christian tradition that includes room for hope as well as the fear of eternal damnation.

The Black Swan

Thomas Mann's last novella was also one of his most controversial. *Die Betrogene* (literally, "The Deceived Woman," translated as *The Black Swan*, 1953) focuses on themes that seem calculated to make readers of the 1950s uncomfortable: can a post-menopausal woman experience sexual desire? Is it appropriate for an older woman to fall in love with a man who could be her son? *The Black Swan* begins in the deliberately archaic style of an old-fashioned storyteller – Mann reread Heinrich von Kleist's novellas as he was preparing to write *The Black Swan* – who refers with tongue-in-cheek humor to the frequent infidelity of the protagonist's deceased husband as only a symptom of his lust for life, but it ends with a clinical description of uterine cancer at an advanced and inoperable stage.

On April 6, 1952 Mann noted in his diary that Katia had recalled a story at breakfast that morning about an older woman from Munich who falls passionately in love with her son's young tutor. To her surprise and delight, the woman has what seems to be her first period in years, which she understands as a sign of renewed vitality. But her body has deceived her: the bleeding was in fact a symptom of uterine cancer. Mann records the anecdote at some length in his diary, suggesting that he was already thinking of basing a novella on this curious incident (Goethe defined the genre of the novella as a story that focuses on an "unerhörte Begebenheit," literally, an "unheard-of event" – that is, an occurrence without precedent that has nevertheless actually happened). On May 5, Mann wrote to his doctor, Frederick Rosenthal, for information about the disease, which he gladly provided, and on May 14, he noted that he had written the first lines of the novella. Mann was still living in California, but in late June he and Katia flew back to Europe for what turned out to be the last time. Progress on the novella was disrupted by frequent travel that summer and fall, and a bad case of bronchitis in the winter, but by March 18, 1953 it was finished. "Well, then, I've managed to complete that, too," noted Mann with evident satisfaction, commenting that the novella marked a new direction in his work and that it was "beautiful and strange" (*ein schönes, merkwürdiges Werk*).

Although *The Black Swan* is ostensibly about a woman in her early fifties, it is easy to read it as another piece of masked autobiography. Doctor Rosenthal was the man who had correctly diagnosed Mann's lung cancer in 1946, and it is not surprising that Mann's thoughts turned to disease and death in what turned out to be his final novella – although he had of course been writing about disease and death for his entire career! The story takes place in Düsseldorf, the home of Klaus Heuser, a young man to whom Mann had been passionately attracted in the summer of 1927 when he was about the same age as the protagonist of *The Black Swan*, Frau Rosalie von Tümmler. She falls in love with a twenty-four-year-old American, Ken Keaton. As in the case of Mut-em-enet's attraction to Joseph and Madame Houpflé's passion for Felix Krull, Rosalie von Tümmler's interest in the broad-shouldered, slender-hipped Ken Keaton allowed Mann to write about homosexual desire under the camouflage of heterosexual passion.

The novella is set in about 1925. Rosalie's husband had died at the beginning of the First World War when she was forty years old. The widow lives with her daughter, Anna, an avant-garde artist with a club foot who is on the verge of being an old maid at twenty-nine, and son of eighteen, Eduard, who takes English lessons with Ken Keaton in the hope of improving his chances in the business world. Unlike her intellectually gifted but physically handicapped daughter, Rosalie is a well-preserved woman with lively brown eyes. She enjoys a glass of wine with good company and can be moved to rapture by the smell of a rose or a walk through the woods. Rosalie gradually becomes infatuated with Ken and finally kisses him passionately during a visit to an old castle by the Rhine. She promises to come to him that evening, but is instead stricken with heavy bleeding and taken to the hospital. As in Katia Mann's anecdote, what Rosalie von Tümmler thought was renewed menstruation is a symptom of the cancer that soon kills her.

The Black Swan touches on several themes present elsewhere in Mann's work. Rosalie is another character smitten by a destructive passion. As in *Death in Venice*, sexual desire of a socially questionable sort is linked to disease, death, and the underworld: the red-bearded pilot of the ferry that takes Rosalie and Ken down the Rhine to the castle is another embodiment of Charon, and they kiss in a secret underground passageway that smells of mold and decay. The Oedipal theme of *The Holy Sinner* recurs here as well, as Anna debates at length with her mother the propriety of her attraction to the younger man. Ken Keaton is another embodiment of "Life," a physically appealing caricature of an American who finds Europe charming because it is so old. Despite Mann's apparent focus on feminine or even feminist issues, the depiction of Rosalie and her daughter nevertheless slides toward the misogynist clichés present in his early work: the pairing of a sensual but not particularly bright mother with a club-footed intellectual daughter recalls characters as old as Amra in *Little Louise* and Dunja Stegemann in *Revenged* (*Gerächt*, 1899): the former has a voluptuous body and a vapid mind, the latter has the mind of a philosopher and "the physical charms of a broomstick."

As the novella's title suggests, the theme of deception is central to the work. Nothing is quite what it seems: Herr von Tümmler is said to have died honorably in the war, but in fact he succumbed to a random automobile accident. Ken Keaton is a seemingly vital young man who is having an affair with at least one other older woman, but he was badly wounded in the war and has the use of only one kidney. Rosalie prefers the simple, direct experience of nature to her daughter's Cubist paintings, but nature deceives her in the end. The setting of the novella in 1925 places it in close proximity to the period depicted in *Disorder and Early Sorrow*, and Rosalie justifies her unconventional attraction to the younger man in terms of a general loosening of social mores at the time, but it also reflects indirectly the instability of the post-Second World War period in which it was written. Neither the Old World of Europe nor the New World as represented by Ken Keaton seems particularly admirable or reliable.

The interpretation of the novella hinges to a large extent on Rosalie's last words to her daughter before dying: "never say that nature deceived me, that she is sardonic and cruel."[3] She admits that she dies reluctantly, but insists that death is part of life and that her fleeting sense of rejuvenation was not a lie on the part of nature, but actually an act of goodness and mercy (*Gnade*). Rosalie's words are ambivalent. On the one hand, we can dismiss them as her final deception, a desperate attempt to preserve her optimistic view of nature even when it has tricked her into seeing signs of new life in what were in fact symptoms of a terminal illness. On the other hand, she suggests that the deception was more benevolent than cruel: was it not better to believe, however misguidedly, in the rejuvenating power of love than to know from the start that it is the beginning of the end? From a still larger perspective, what seems like cruel deception from an individual perspective can be affirmed as part of a universe that, in its entirety, is beyond good and evil. Goethe suggests as much in the "Prologue in Heaven" of his *Faust*, and Mann places Goethe in this transcendent position in *Lotte in Weimar*, far above the petty concerns of those who surround him. As Dr. Riemer explains, "for He is the whole" (*Er ist ja das Ganze*) (p. 82). Mann's novella about the deceived woman can thus be read as "a very serious jest," as the aging Goethe once said of his *Faust*, a late work that holds out the tenuous promise of a hope beyond hopelessness, a presentiment of certainty that lies beyond the deceptive appearance of nature.

The *Confessions of Felix Krull*

While Mann occasionally wrote his shorter novellas in a concentrated burst of energy, the composition of his novels was more typically interrupted for months or even years by other projects. *The Magic Mountain* had lain fallow for half a decade during the First World War, and he paused four years after completing *Joseph in Egypt* before beginning work on *Joseph the Provider*. The *Confessions of Felix Krull* breaks all records in this regard, however, for Mann waited until he was in his late seventies to resume work on a project that he had begun in his thirties. The work was conceived in the summer of 1909, shortly after Mann had completed *Royal Highness*. He began work in earnest the following winter and by July 1910 he was able to read the first chapter aloud to his family. Work on *Felix Krull* continued intermittently over the next few years, interrupted by *Death in Venice* and the earliest portions of *The Magic Mountain*, but the war stopped all progress for decades. Mann never forgot about the project, however: he had published the section about Krull's visit to the theater already in 1911, and he published longer sections of the novel's opening books in the early 1920s and again in 1937. In the spring of 1943, Mann considered taking up the novel again, but decided to focus on *Doctor Faustus* instead. Only in January 1951, after he had completed *The Holy Sinner*, did Mann finally resume work on the *Confessions of Felix Krull*. Contrary to his usual practice, however, he decided to leave this work a fragment. After publishing what he termed "part one" of *Felix Krull* in September 1954, he turned his remaining energy to his long Schiller essay. Plans for a drama about *Luther's Wedding* (*Luthers Hochzeit*) were interrupted by his death.

The *Confessions of Felix Krull* is a fictional autobiography, the memoires of a con-man apparently written in prison, although we learn nothing of the events that led to his arrest in the existing fragment. In terms of style and genre, the work parodies Goethe's autobiography, *Poetry and Truth*, and once again has ties to the genre of the *Bildungsroman*, following as it does the protagonist's career from his birth in a village along the Rhine, his move to Frankfurt with his mother and sister after his father's death, and his adventures in Paris as a waiter in the Hotel Saint James and Albany. Krull embarks on a journey around the world, posing as the Marquis de Venosta, but he only makes it as far as Portugal before the novel breaks off. Unlike the typical hero of a *Bildungsroman*, however, Felix Krull undergoes no character development and displays none of the brooding introspection that makes Goethe's Wilhelm Meister a kindred spirit of Hamlet. Krull is serenely confident in his innate superiority and glides effortlessly through a series of adventures in a manner more typical of the picaresque novel.

The theme of the artist as a charlatan recurs frequently in Mann's early work. The transparently autobiographical *Bajazzo* paints a portrait of the artist as a young dilettante; Tonio Kröger tells Lisaweta that the artist is the brother of the criminal and then nearly gets arrested in a case of mistaken identity when he returns to his hometown; *Das Wunderkind* depicts a gifted child whose crowd-pleasing virtuosity leaves the skeptical narrator unconvinced. Krull's visit to the theater follows the same pattern: the actor Müller-Rosé transfixes the audience with his charm, but turns out to be depressingly ordinary backstage. Such stories reflect an element of self-criticism, as Mann worries that his desire to appeal simultaneously to "stupid" readers as well as the critical elite may make him guilty of pandering to the masses. Elsewhere, Mann directs his venom against others whom he accuses of trying to dash off sensational novels (Heinrich Mann) or to compose melodramatic music calculated to enrapture an undiscerning audience (Richard Wagner). Even Gustav von Aschenbach, the champion of an anti-sentimental, rigorously modern prose, comes to the conclusion that his chiseled style is based on a lie and that his highly praised works are unworthy of respect.

Felix Krull suffers no such torment. Convinced of the bedrock truth of his own superiority, he delights in living the lie, in playing roles ranging from attentive waiter to elegant aristocrat. On his train ride to Portugal, Professor Kuckuck tells him that this world is merely a fleeting moment between the nothingness that preceded creation and that nothingness that is sure to follow, but rather than despairing at the transitory nature of our existence and the world around us, Felix Krull delights in its beauty – beginning with his own handsome body. Mann referred to the *Confessions of Felix Krull* as his "homosexual novel" in a diary entry of November 25, 1950, and his slender, bronze-skinned young hero with blond hair and gray-blue eyes conforms to a physical type that had always attracted him. Krull accepts matter-of-factly that men as well as women find him irresistible – as he coyly puts it, he can hardly condemn as unnatural sexual desires inspired by his charming appearance. Krull's night of riotous sex with Madame Diane Houpflé, who enjoys being humiliated by the "stupid little slave" who stole her jewelry,[4] is as close as Mann got to describing a homosexual fantasy in his fiction – disguised, of course, as a heterosexual encounter. As Mann's narrator puts it in *The Holy Sinner*, "very oft is the telling only a substitute for enjoyment which we, or the heavens, deny ourselves" (p. 160).

On a mythological level, Felix Krull is the embodiment of Hermes, the god of thieves, and Narcissus, the self-absorbed beauty. Professor Kuckuck adds philosophical depth to the later portions of the *Confessions*, as his description of the transitory nature of creation recalls Schopenhauer's belief – together with the Hindu philosophy that inspired it – that this world is mere "maya," a veil of illusion stretched over the void. Thomas Buddenbrook tried to turn this pessimism into a Nietzschean affirmation of life before being felled by his infected tooth, but Felix Krull experiences no sense of crisis, philosophical or otherwise. He is a political conservative, not because he is born to the manor like Klaus Heinrich of *Royal Highness*, but because he finds the world so delightful as it is that there is no reason to change anything. In addition to enjoying fine food, expensive jewelry, and well-tailored clothing, Krull also enjoys observing attractive people, particularly if they are marked by a touch of racial or ethnic difference. Felix Krull receives his sexual initiation through Rosza, another Hungarian prostitute like Leverkühn's Hetaera Esmeralda – although Krull finds sex delightful, whereas Leverkühn seems to view it only as an unpleasant means to the end of contracting syphilis. He comments

repeatedly on the racial mixture of the Portuguese that has resulted from centuries of conquest and being conquered, and is particularly fascinated by an
exotic young couple that he sees from a distance in Frankfurt (Mann's notes
for the unwritten continuation of the novel indicate that they are children of
a Venezuelan woman whom Krull was to have met again in Argentina). In a
sense, Krull's planned journey from Portugal to South America is a symbolic
homecoming for Mann, a final vicarious return to his mother's origins and the
theme of racial stigma and distinction that runs through his work.

Mann was plagued by doubts when he resumed work on the *Confessions of
Felix Krull* after so many years. He wondered if it was appropriate to devote
his waning energies to a frivolous book about the erotic adventures of a young
man, and he worried that it would be rejected by his readers. "I fear a humiliating reception of the Krull-volume," he noted in his diary on June 4, 1954,
"and I don't know how I am supposed to find a new project. I am so worried about the rest of my life." To his surprise and delight, the *Confessions of
Felix Krull* turned out to be his most popular and critically acclaimed work
in years. For the last time, Mann's tactic of the "double optic" had succeeded
after all.

Mann's subsequent reception and reputation

Mann's life ended shortly after a series of public events in celebration of his
eightieth birthday, and after his death he continued to be hailed as the most
important German writer of the twentieth century and the last great man of
European letters. Erika Mann set the tone with an idealized account of her
father's final year (*Das letzte Jahr*, 1956) and devoted the rest of her life to edit-
ing his correspondence and defending his reputation. Once the contentious
author was safely in his grave, it was easier for the general public to embrace
his memory. As Henry Hatfield put it in the Foreword to his revised introduction to Thomas Mann (originally published in 1951), "the Germans have at
last forgiven Mann for having been right about Hitler."[5] For postwar professors
and students of German literature, Mann was an inexhaustible treasure trove.
T. J. Reed noted in the introduction to his landmark study, *Thomas Mann: The
Uses of Tradition* (1974), that Mann wrote "the kind of work, and with his personal background and image he was the kind of writer, to make academics feel
at home."[6] No stone was left unturned. Articles and monographs unearthed
Mann's sources, explored his relationship with Goethe, pondered with great
seriousness the nature of his humor, and sifted through his views on music,
philosophy, psychology, mythology, and theology.

Not everyone shared the enthusiasm. While the critical industry surrounding Mann was running at full capacity, radical students of the 1960s were growing increasingly impatient with cultural icons such as Mann. While Kafka's mysterious fiction touched a nerve among a generation of seekers and Brecht's uncompromising communism inspired political activists, Mann seemed old-fashioned, to be respected perhaps as a relic of a bygone age, but a writer with no contemporary relevance. A series of interviews with writers from both East and West Germany published in the journal *Text + Kritik* in 1976 captured Mann's reputation at its nadir. While a few authors managed polite comments about Mann's work, the general mood oscillated between indifference and open hostility. No, I never read Thomas Mann, responded one author after the next, and he had no influence on my work. Others were more aggressive. Reinhard Lettau castigated Mann as an affected prima donna, a high school dropout who spent a lifetime serving up watered-down, misunderstood romanticism to his sycophantic readers. Rolf Schneider accused him of political opportunism and clandestine anti-Semitism. Peter Rühmkorf complained that Mann's precious style made him feel almost physically ill. Still others lamented that excessive critical attention to Thomas Mann had eclipsed the reputation of other, far more deserving writers.

Reports of Mann's demise were premature; his public profile in the early twenty-first century seems higher than ever. Mann's works are readily available in inexpensive editions throughout the German-speaking world, new translations of the major novels into English by John E. Woods have received glowing reviews, and a major new critical edition is underway. Mann's continuing ability to appeal to a general, educated public lies in part in the relative accessibility of his work, as opposed to that of more avant-garde modernists, but also in his immense cultural cache. The vehemence with which writers rejected Mann in the 1970s can be read as an indirect testimony to his prestige. The more recent boom in Mann studies may reflect a certain mellowing toward figures of cultural authority or, if you will, a reactionary backlash. But the most vital Mann scholarship of the past decades has not been motivated by a misguided desire to place a fallen idol back on his pedestal, but rather by the perceived need to engage critically with an artist and public intellectual of lasting importance despite – and also because – of his flaws as well as his accomplishments. Thomas Mann today is still admired and reviled, but not ignored.

The gradual publication of Mann's diaries between the years 1977 and 1995 has revitalized the study of the man and his work. Mann's decision to reveal his intimate diaries to the public was the final manifestation of the confessional impulse that had been present throughout his life, a tendency that he shared with other family members. Shortly before his death, Mann's youngest brother,

Viktor, surprised everyone with a highly readable, if not entirely accurate, portrait of his family (*Wir waren fünf,* 1949). Heinrich Mann also published his memoires late in life, while Klaus Mann began writing his autobiography at the ridiculously early age of twenty-six. Nearly all of Klaus' siblings also published some sort of autobiographical work; Mann's grandson Frido has now added to the collection. Only Katia had to be coaxed into dictating her *Unwritten Memories* when she was in her nineties, because, as she put it, "there must be one person in this family who doesn't write" (p. ix).

The autobiographical eruption has been followed by a biographical tsunami. No less than five major biographies of Thomas Mann appeared between 1995 and 1999, all drawing extensively on information revealed in the diaries. Biographical studies of either the extended Mann family or particular family members have also proliferated in recent decades. Examples of the former include Marcel Reich-Ranicki's *Thomas Mann und die Seinen* (Thomas Mann and his Family, 1987), Marianne Krüll's *Im Netz der Zauberer* (In the Net of the Magicians, 1991), and the made-for-television docudrama *Die Manns: Ein Jahrhundertroman* (The Family Mann: A Novel of the Century, 2003), with the well-known actor Armin Müller-Stahl in the role of Thomas Mann. Biographies of Mann's immediate family members, including Heinrich, Katia, Erika, Klaus, and Golo, have been followed by portraits of individuals increasingly peripheral to the life of Thomas Mann, although of course interesting in their own right. Examples include Inge and Walter Jens' portrait of Hedwig Pringsheim (*Katias Mutter,* 2007) and Kirsten Jüngling's biography of Nelly Mann, Heinrich's third wife and the target of Thomas Mann's open and undying hatred, under the somewhat apologetic title *Ich bin doch nicht nur schlecht* (I'm not only bad, after all, 2009).

Clearly there is money to be made in the business of the Mann family biography. But it is not only the desire for profit that is fueling the current interest in the "amazing family." Biographies of individual family members often have an axe to grind, as they turn sympathetic portraits of Mann's supposedly neglected or abused children into indictments of the father. Biographers of Thomas Mann tend to be more sympathetic, with the notable exception of Klaus Harpprecht, whose 2,200-page tome is relentlessly critical of nearly everything that Mann said and did. When Mann's diaries were initially released, some readers complained that they contain too many trivial details, but the biographers know that it is intrinsically interesting to peek behind the curtains of a life performed in public, particularly when the individual has been on stage for so long during such turbulent times.

The publication of the diaries has also given new impetus to scholars seeking insight into Mann's literary works and his creative process. For instance, scattered comments about the Jews in the diaries have rekindled old contro-versies about alleged anti-Semitism in Mann's life and works. While some have condemned the man and others defend him, a growing number of critics have sought to understand the role of Jewish figures in Mann's fiction in the context of his ambivalent self-image and his portrayal of other stigmatized characters in his work. Heinrich Detering's *Juden, Frauen und Litteraten* (2005) is a par-ticularly sensitive study in this regard; also noteworthy are the two books by Yahya Elsaghe, *Die imaginäre Nation* (2000) and *Thomas Mann und die kleinen Unterschiede* (Small Differences) (2004). My own *Thomas Mann's World* (2010) seeks to place Mann's response to the "Jewish question" in the larger context of his attentiveness toward racial difference in an era of imperial conquest and global conflict.

The most sensational revelation of Mann's diaries was the extent of his homosexual desires. In retrospect, this should not have been such a surprise: from Tonio Kröger's love for Hans Hansen through Gustav von Aschenbach's infatuation with Tadzio to Hans Castorp's attraction to Pribislav Hippe, male–male desire plays a central role in Mann's fiction. Many of Mann's contempor-aries suspected that there was something queer about his sexual orientation, beginning with Heinrich, who had once suggested to his then-teenage brother that a session or two with a good prostitute would resolve his sexual confusion; in later years, Katia and Erika were well aware of Mann's fondness for hand-some young men. Nevertheless, the public admission of homosexuality was taboo throughout Mann's lifetime, and besides, he had a wife and six children to prove that he was "normal." Mann's frank confessions in his diaries forced readers to confront an issue that many would have preferred to leave quietly in the closet. To some, Mann's sexual orientation was a private matter that had nothing to do with his fiction or role as a public intellectual. Those who drew attention to the more sensational passages in the diaries were motivated only by prurient interest, in this view, or perhaps by a belated desire to slander the master.

Increasingly, however, a consensus has emerged that questions of sexuality and gender are of central importance to understanding Thomas Mann and his works. Herman Kurzke has argued convincingly that the sublimation of homo-sexual desire was one of the key motivating factors in Mann's art. Anthony Heilbut celebrates Mann as a great homosexual writer, stressing again and again the importance of same-sex desire in Mann's life and work. Mann's pre-occupation with male–male desire and the moments of misogyny in his work may stem from his personal sexual orientation, but they also participate in widespread debates among his contemporaries about the nature of sexual dif-ference and the proper organization of society. Thus Mann's work has become a source of renewed interest among those who explore gender roles in modern fiction and the sexual politics of the modern state.

These recent studies of gender and Jewishness in Mann's fiction reflect a larger move away from the formalist literary studies that dominated postwar criticism toward an understanding of literature in social and biographical context. If the danger of formalist criticism lay in its tendency to place works on a magic mountain, far above the mundane concerns of those toiling in the flatlands, the threat of more recent cultural studies lies in the disenchantment of literary magic, the reduction of the aesthetic object to brute historical facts and biographical trivia. The nature of Mann's fiction suggests the necessity for a middle course between these caricatured extremes. Self-consciously literary and yet historically grounded, intimately confessional and yet publicly representative, Mann's work requires a critical understanding of his life and times, but also rewards readers who appreciate subtly drawn characters, a compelling plot, and a sense of humor. Mann lived a tormented life in turbulent times; he bore the self-imposed weight of Germany's destiny on his shoulders; but he was also an entertainer who strove in his literary works to keep magic on the mountain.

Notes

1 Introduction

1 Heinrich Mann, *Die beiden Gesichter* (*Both Faces*, 1929) in *Das Kind: Geschichten aus der Familie*, ed. Kerstin Schneider (Frankfurt am Main: Fischer, 2001), pp. 14–18.
2 *Death in Venice and Other Stories by Thomas Mann*, trans. David Luke (New York: Bantam, 1988), p. 138.
3 Jürgen Habermas, *The Structural Transformation of the Public Sphere: An Inquiry into a Category of Bourgeois Society*, trans. Thomas Burger (Cambridge, MA: MIT Press, 1989), pp. 5–14.
4 Fritz Stern, *The Politics of Cultural Despair: A Study in the Rise of the Germanic Ideology* (Berkeley: University of California Press, 1961).
5 Anthony Heilbut, *Thomas Mann: Eros and Literature* (Berkeley: University of California Press, 1995), p. 251.
6 Katia Mann, *Unwritten Memories*, trans. Hunter and Hildegarde Hannum (New York: Knopf, 1975), p. 45.
7 Thomas Mann, *Ansprache in Lübeck* (*Address in Lübeck*, 1955) in Thomas Mann, *Gesammelte Werke*, 13 vols. (Frankfurt am Main: Fischer, 1960–74), vol. 11, pp. 533–36. When possible, references to Mann's essays will be to this edition, henceforth referred to by the abbreviation *GW* followed by volume and page number.
8 Klaus Mann, *The Turning Point* (New York: Markus Wiener, 1984), pp. 7–8.
9 Thomas Mann, *Joseph and his Brothers*, trans. John E. Woods (New York: Knopf, 2005), p. 882.
10 Thomas Mann, *Royal Highness*, trans. A. Cecil Curtis (Berkeley: University of California Press, 1992), p. 338.

2 Origins, influences, and early mastery

1 Thomas Mann, *Erkenne Dich Selbst!* (*Know Yourself!*, 1895) in Thomas Mann, *Essays*, 6 vols., ed. Hermann Kurzke and Stephan Stachorski (Frankfurt am Main: Fischer, 1993–97), vol. 1, pp. 16–17. Hereafter cited as *Essays* followed by volume and page number.

128

2 Thomas Mann, *Buddenbrooks*, trans. John E. Woods (New York: Knopf, 1993), p. 563.
3 Thomas Mann, *Leiden und Größe Richard Wagners* (*Suffering and Greatness of Richard Wagner*, 1933). *GW* vol. 9, pp. 363–426.
4 Quoted from Manfred Flügge, *Heinrich Mann: Eine Biographie* (Reinbek bei Hamburg: Rowohlt, 2006), p. 46.
5 Klaus Theweleit, *Male Fantasies*, trans. Erica Carter, Stephen Conway, and Chris Turner (Minneapolis: University of Minnesota Press, 1987–89).
6 Georg Lukács, *Thomas Mann* (Berlin: Aufbau, 1949).
7 Martin Swales, *Buddenbrooks: Family Life as the Mirror of Social Change* (Boston: Twayne, 1991).
8 Ernest M. Wolf, "Hagenströms: The Rival Family in Thomas Mann's *Buddenbrooks*," *German Studies Review* 5 (1982): 35–55.
9 Yahya Elsaghe, *Die imaginäre Nation: Thomas Mann und das "Deutsche"* (Munich: Fink, 2000), pp. 188–205. Hermann Kurzke defends Mann against charges of anti-Semitism in *Thomas Mann: Life as a Work of Art: A Biography*, trans. Leslie Willson (Princeton University Press, 2002), pp. 187–214.

3 Artists and outcasts in Mann's early fiction

1 Quoted from Manfred Flügge, *Heinrich Mann*, p. 96.
2 Thomas Mann, *Tonio Kröger* in *Death in Venice and Other Stories*, trans. David Luke (New York: Bantam, 1988), p. 152.
3 Thomas Mann, *Gladius Dei* in *Death in Venice and Other Stories*, p. 89.
4 Thomas Mann, *Tristan* in *Death in Venice and Other Stories*, p. 94.
5 "Ganev" means thief in Yiddish. "Beganeft" is actually an incorrect past participle that Mann allegedly learned from his father-in-law, Alfred Pringsheim, when seeking a word that would provide the appropriate ethnic flair for the conclusion to his story. In context it means that the twins have stolen the bride's virginity in advance of the wedding.
6 Thomas Mann, *Royal Highness*, p. 338.
7 Katia Mann, *Unwritten Memories*, p. 58.
8 Katia Mann, *Unwritten Memories*, pp. 61–65.
9 Thomas Mann, *Death in Venice* in *Death in Venice and Other Stories*, p. 200. Hereafter cited in the text.
10 Hermann Kurzke, *Thomas Mann: Life as a Work of Art*, pp. 196–98.
11 Edward Said, *Orientalism* (New York: Vintage, 1979).
12 Stephan Besser, "Die hygienische Eroberung Afrikas" in *Mit Deutschland um die Welt: Eine Kulturgeschichte des Fremden in der Kolonialzeit*, ed. Alexander Honold and Klaus R. Scherpe (Stuttgart: Metzler, 2004), pp. 217–25.

4 From world war to the Weimar Republic

1 Klaus Mann, *The Turning Point* (New York: Markus Wiener, 1984), pp. 38–39.
2 Thomas Mann, *Reflections of a Nonpolitical Man*, trans. Walter D. Morris (New York: Unger, 1983), p. 98.
3 Both terms appear in the essay "Zum Geleit" (Preface, 1921) in Thomas Mann, *Essays*, vol. 2, pp. 30–42.
4 Thomas Mann, "An Jakob Wassermann" (To Jakob Wassermann, 1921). *GW* vol. 13, pp. 463–65.
5 William Arctander O'Brien, *Novalis: Signs of Revolution* (Durham and London: Duke University Press, 1995).
6 Thomas Mann, *The Magic Mountain*, trans. John E. Woods (New York: Random House, 1995), p. xi.
7 Katia Mann, *Unwritten Memories*, pp. 68–76.
8 Hermann Weigand, *Thomas Mann's Novel "Der Zauberberg": A Study* (New York: Appleton-Century, 1933), p. 5.

5 The struggle against National Socialism

1 Thomas Mann, *Die Juden werden dauern!* (The Jews Will Survive, 1936). *Essays*, vol. 4, pp. 177–78.
2 Thomas Mann, *Pariser Rechenschaft* (Parisian Account, 1926). *GW* vol. 11, pp. 9–97.
3 Thomas Mann, *Goethe als Repräsentant des bürgerlichen Zeitalters* (Goethe as a Representative of the Bourgeois Age). *GW* vol. 9, pp. 297–332.
4 *Deutsche Hörer!* (German Listeners, January 1942). Thomas Mann, *Deutsche Hörer! Radiosendungen nach Deutschland aus den Jahren 1940–1945* (Frankfurt am Main: Fischer, 1987), pp. 49–52.
5 Thomas Mann, *Disorder and Early Sorrow* in *Death in Venice and Seven Other Stories*, trans. H. T. Lowe-Porter (New York: Knopf, 1963), p. 182. Hereafter cited in the text.
6 *Erinnerungen aus der deutschen Inflation* (Memories of the German Inflation, 1942). *GW* vol. 13, pp. 181–90.
7 Hermann Kurzke, *Thomas Mann: Life as a Work of Art*, p. 417.
8 *Lotte in Weimar*, trans. H. T. Lowe-Porter (New York: Knopf, 1940), p. 71. Hereafter cited in the text.
9 In the autobiographical essay "On Myself" (1940). *GW* vol. 13, pp. 127–69.
10 Letter to Agnes E. Meyer, July 27, 1940.
11 Eve Kosofsky Sedgwick, *Between Men: English Literature and Male Homosexual Desire* (New York: Columbia University Press, 1985).

12 Cited from Hans Rudolf Vaget, *Thomas Mann-Kommentar zu sämtlichen Erzählungen* (Munich: Winkler, 1984), p. 277.

13 *The Tables of the Law*, trans. H. T. Lowe-Porter (New York: Knopf, 1945), p. 7. Hereafter cited in the text.

6 A pact with the devil: *Doctor Faustus*

1 Thomas Mann, *The Story of a Novel: The Genesis of Doctor Faustus*, trans. Richard and Clara Winston (New York: Knopf, 1961), p. 38. Hereafter cited in the text.

2 The old notebook was dated 1901, as Mann notes in *The Story of a Novel*, but recent editors suggest that the actual entry about a Faust-novella dates from approximately 1904.

3 In early editions of *Doctor Faustus*, Zeitblom begins his narrative on May 27, not May 23, 1943. The date has been changed to May 23 in many subsequent editions, including John E. Woods' English translation, to be consistent with *The Story of a Novel* and Mann's diary. The editors of the new standard German edition have chosen to leave the original date of May 27 in the text of the novel, but they note in the commentary that Mann probably overlooked his mistake when correcting the proofs.

4 *Doctor Faustus*, trans. John E. Woods (New York: Random House, 1997), p. 10. Hereafter cited in the text.

5 Gunilla Bergsten, *Thomas Mann's Doctor Faustus: The Sources and Structure of the Novel*, trans. Krishna Winston (University of Chicago Press, 1969).

7 Tribulations and final triumphs

1 *The Holy Sinner*, trans. H. T. Lowe-Porter (New York: Knopf, 1951), p. 133. Hereafter cited in the text.

2 Hermann Kurzke, *Thomas Mann: Life as a Work of Art*, pp. 548–52.

3 *The Black Swan*, trans. Willard R. Trask (New York: Knopf, 1954), p. 140.

4 "Petit esclave stupide," *Confessions of Felix Krull*, trans. Denver Lindley (New York: Knopf, 1955), p. 169.

5 Henry Hatfield, *Thomas Mann* (Norfolk, Connecticut: New Directions, 1962), p. viii.

6 T. J. Reed, *Thomas Mann: The Uses of Tradition* (Oxford: Clarendon Press, 1974), p. 2.

Suggested further reading

The secondary literature on Thomas Mann is vast, primarily in German, and often aimed at the specialist. The following list of suggestions for further reading, in contrast, is limited in scope, in English, and accessible to a general reader. Those who are able to read Mann in the original German and want to study his works in greater detail should begin with the excellent new critical edition of his works, the *Große kommentierte Frankfurter Ausgabe*, which has been appearing gradually since 2002. Each of Mann's works is accompanied by extensive critical commentary by a leading scholar, together with a substantial, up-to-date bibliography.

Novels

Buddenbrooks: The Decline of a Family (1901). Trans. John E. Woods. New York: Knopf, 1993.
Royal Highness (1909). Trans. A. Cecil Curtis. New York: Knopf, 1939.
The Magic Mountain (1924). Trans. John E. Woods. New York: Knopf, 1995.
Joseph and his Brothers (1933–43). Trans. John E. Woods. New York: Knopf, 2005.
The Beloved Returns: Lotte in Weimar (1939). Trans. H. T. Lowe-Porter. New York: Knopf, 1940.
Doctor Faustus (1947). Trans. John E. Woods. New York: Knopf, 1997.
The Holy Sinner (1951). Trans. H. T. Lowe-Porter. New York: Knopf, 1951.
Confessions of Felix Krull, Confidence Man (The Early Years) (1954). Trans. Denver Lindley. New York: Knopf, 1955.

Selected stories

Death in Venice and Seven Other Stories. Trans. H. T. Lowe-Porter. New York: Knopf, 1963.
Death in Venice and Other Stories by Thomas Mann. Trans. David Luke. New York: Bantam, 1988.

The Tables of the Law (1943). Trans. H. T. Lowe-Porter. New York: Knopf, 1945.
The Black Swan (1953). Trans. Willard R. Trask. New York: Knopf, 1954.

Essays, diaries, and letters

Order of the Day: Political Essays and Speeches of Two Decades. Trans. H. T. Lowe-
     Porter. New York: Knopf, 1942.
The Story of a Novel: The Genesis of Doctor Faustus. Trans. Richard and Clara
     Winston. New York: Knopf, 1961.
Letters of Thomas Mann 1889–1955 (selections). New York: Knopf, 1971.
Thomas Mann: Diaries 1918–1939 (selections). New York: Abrams, 1982.
Reflections of a Nonpolitical Man. Trans. Walter D. Morris. New York: Ungar,
     1983.
Death in Venice, Tonio Kröger, and Other Writings. Ed. Frederick A. Lubich. New
     York: Continuum, 1999.

Memoires

Erika Mann. *The Last Year of Thomas Mann.* New York: Farrar, Straus and
     Cudahy, 1958.
Katia Mann. *Unwritten Memories.* New York: Knopf, 1975.
Klaus Mann. *The Turning Point.* New York: Wiener, 1984.

Selected critical analyses

Ruth Angress-Klüger. "Jewish Characters in Thomas Mann's Fiction." *Horizonte:
     Festschrift für Herbert Lehnert zum 65. Geburtstag.* Eds. Hannelore
     Mundt, Egon Schwarz, and William J. Lillymann. Tübingen: Niemeyer,
     1990, pp. 161–72. Incisive, frequently cited article.
Gunilla Bergsten. *Thomas Mann's Doctor Faustus: The Sources and Structure of the
     Novel.* 1963; University of Chicago Press, 1969. Essential introduction
     to Mann's "montage-technique." Documents many sources for *Doctor
     Faustus.*
Stephen D. Dowden, ed. *A Companion to Thomas Mann's The Magic Mountain.*
     Columbia, South Carolina: Camden House, 1999. Includes an important
     article by Kenneth Weisinger and a fascinating autobiographical account
     of Susan Sontag's meeting with Thomas Mann.
Henry Hatfield. *Thomas Mann.* 1951; New York: New Directions, 1962. Succinct,
     highly readable, and astute.

Henry Hatfield. *From the Magic Mountain: Mann's Later Masterpieces.*
    Ithaca: Cornell University Press, 1979. A more focused study of the
    second half of Mann's career.
Anthony Heilbut. *Thomas Mann: Eros and Literature.* Berkeley: University of
    California Press, 1995. Lively prose style, stresses Mann's homosexuality.
    Primary focus on Mann's early works through *The Magic Mountain.*
Erich Heller. *Thomas Mann: The Ironic German.* 1958; revised New York:
    Cambridge University Press, 1981. Stresses Schopenhauer's influence.
Todd Kontje. *Thomas Mann's World: Empire, Race, and the Jewish Question.* Ann
    Arbor: University of Michigan Press, 2010. Views Mann's conflicted
    response to the "Jewish question" in the larger context of his attitude
    toward racial difference in an age of empire and global conflict.
Hermann Kurzke. *Thomas Mann: Life as a Work of Art: A Biography.* 1998; trans.
    Leslie Willson. Princeton University Press, 2002. Sympathetic, sensitive,
    authoritative biography by one of Germany's leading Mann scholars.
    Full of crucial insights into the man and his works.
Donald Prater. *Thomas Mann: A Life.* Oxford University Press, 1995. Even-
    handed, authoritative account of Mann's life.
T. J. Reed. *Thomas Mann: The Uses of Tradition.* 1974; revised edition
    Oxford: Clarendon, 1996. Standard work stresses genesis of individual
    texts and their place in literary-historical tradition. Also good on
    Mann's political evolution.
Ritchie Robertson, ed. *The Cambridge Companion to Thomas Mann.* Cambridge
    University Press, 2002. An excellent anthology of essays by leading
    Mann scholars.
Martin Swales. *Thomas Mann: A Study.* London: Heinemann, 1980. Good brief
    overview.
Martin Swales. *Buddenbrooks: Family Life as the Mirror of Social Change.*
    Boston: Twayne, 1991. Detailed study of Mann's first novel in historical
    and biographical context.
Hans Rudolf Vaget, ed. *Thomas Mann's The Magic Mountain: A Casebook.* Oxford
    University Press, 2008. Thought-provoking essays by recent Mann
    scholars.
Hermann J. Weigand. *Thomas Mann's Novel "Der Zauberberg": A Study.* New
    York: Appleton-Century, 1933. A landmark of early Thomas Mann
    criticism that places *The Magic Mountain* in the context of Mann's early
    career and German literary history.

Index

Cambridge Introductions to ...

AUTHORS

Margaret Atwood Heidi Macpherson

Jane Austen Janet Todd

Samuel Beckett Ronan McDonald

Walter Benjamin David Ferris

Chekhov James N. Loehlin

J. M. Coetzee Dominic Head

Samuel Taylor Coleridge John Worthen

Joseph Conrad John Peters

Jacques Derrida Leslie Hill

Charles Dickens Jon Mee

Emily Dickinson Wendy Martin

George Eliot Nancy Henry

T. S. Eliot John Xiros Cooper

William Faulkner Theresa M. Towner

F. Scott Fitzgerald Kirk Curnutt

Michel Foucault Lisa Downing

Robert Frost Robert Faggen

Nathaniel Hawthorne Leland S. Person

Zora Neale Hurston Lovalerie King

James Joyce Eric Bulson

Thomas Mann Todd Kontje

Herman Melville Kevin J. Hayes

Sylvia Plath Jo Gill

Edgar Allan Poe Benjamin F. Fisher

Ezra Pound Ira Nadel

Marcel Proust Adam Watt

Jean Rhys Elaine Savory

Edward Said Conor McCarthy

Shakespeare Emma Smith

Shakespeare's Comedies Penny Gay

Shakespeare's History Plays Warren Chernaik

Shakespeare's Poetry Michael Schoenfeldt

Shakespeare's Tragedies Janette Dillon

Harriet Beecher Stowe Sarah Robbins

Mark Twain Peter Messent

Edith Wharton Pamela Knights

Walt Whitman M. Jimmie Killingsworth

Virginia Woolf Jane Goldman

William Wordsworth Emma Mason

W. B. Yeats David Holdeman

TOPICS

The American Short Story Martin Scofield

Comedy Eric Weitz

Creative Writing David Morley

Early English Theatre Janette Dillon

English Theatre, 1660–1900 Peter Thomson

Francophone Literature Patrick Corcoran

Literature and the Environment Timothy Clark

Modern British Theatre Simon Shepherd

Modern Irish Poetry Justin Quinn

Modernism Pericles Lewis

Narrative (second edition) H. Porter Abbott

The Nineteenth-Century American Novel Gregg Crane

The Novel Marina MacKay

Old Norse Sagas Margaret Clunies Ross

CPSIA information can be obtained
at www.ICGtesting.com
Printed in the USA
LVHW091524210719
624773LV00004B/517/P